LIFE SKILLS
AND
TEST PREP
1

Theresa Warren

with Maria H. Koonce

PEARSON
Longman

Life Skills and Test Prep 1

Pearson Education, 10 Bank Street, White Plains, NY 10606

Acknowledgments: The authors wish to acknowledge with gratitude the following reviewers who helped shape the content and approach of *Life Skills and Test Prep 1*: Ronna Magy, LAUSD—Division of Adult and Career Education, Los Angeles, CA • Dr. G. Santos, The English Center, Miami, FL • Edith Uber, Santa Clara Adult Education, Santa Clara, CA • Merari L. Weber, Metropolitan Skills Center, Glendale Community College, Los Angeles, CA.

Staff credits: The people who made up the *Life Skills and Test Prep 1* team, representing editorial, production, design, and manufacturing, are Maretta Callahan, Tracey Cataldo, Dave Dickey, Christine Edmonds, Irene Frankel, Judy Li, Martha McGaughey, Marcia Schonzeit, and Jane Townsend.

Cover Image: José Ortega c/o theispot.com
Text composition: ElectraGraphics, Inc.
Text font: 11 pt Minion
Illustrations: Steve Attoe: pp. 4, 7, 14, 15, 19, 30, 43, 44 (middle), 48, 55, 74, 76, 80 (middle), 96, 99, 100 (middle), 120 (bottom), 136 (top), 140, 142, 145, 146, 149 (top), 150 (bottom), 151 (top), 152 (top), 157, 160, 162, 167, 173, 176, 177, 178, 186, 188, 189, 190, 195; Andy Myer: pp. 2, 8 (top), 16, 34, 61, 95 (bottom), 125, 130 (bottom), 133, 153, 192; George Thompson: p. 193; Gary Torrisi: pp. 38, 39, 41, 47, 72, 73, 80 (top), 81, 82, 83, 95 (top), 98, 108, 116, 118, 120 (top), 121, 123, 130 (top and middle), 131, 132, 164, 165, 168, 170, 171, 172, 174; Wiliam Waitzman: pp. 6, 8 (bottom), 22, 36, 37, 51, 79 (top), 93, 106, 109, 114, 115, 122, 136 (bottom), 138, 143, 148, 149 (bottom), 150 (top), 151 (bottom), 152 (bottom), 158, 159, 169, 182.
Technical art: Tinge Design Studio

Library of Congress Cataloging-in-Publication Data
Warren, Theresa.
   Life skills and test prep 1 / Theresa Warren, with Maria H. Koonce.
     p. cm.
ISBN 978-0-13-199177-4 (student book)
1. English language—Textbooks for foreign speakers. 2. English language—Examinations—Study guides. 3. Life skills—Problems, exercises, etc. I. Koonce, Maria H. II. Title.
PE1128.W36 2007
428.2'4—dc22

                             2007000560

ISBN-13: 978-0-13-199177-4
ISBN-10: 0-13-199177-9

LONGMAN ON THE **WEB**

Longman.com offers online resources for teachers and students. Access our Companion Websites, our online catalog, and our local offices around the world.

Visit us at **longman.com.**

Printed in the United States of America

1 2 3 4 5 6 7 8 9 10–VHG–11 10 09 08 07

Contents

Correlations

Unit 1: Meeting New People	CASAS*	LAUSD**	Florida***
Lesson 1: Introducing Yourself	0.1.4, 0.2.1	1, 9a, 9b	2.05.01
Lesson 2: Introducing a Friend	0.1.1, 0.1.4, 0.2.1	1, 9a, 9b	2.05.01
Lesson 3: Using *Mr., Ms., Mrs.,* and *Miss*	0.1.2, 0.1.4, 0.2.1	1, 9a, 9c	2.05.01
Lesson 4: Family	0.1.2, 0.2.1	6	2.14.01
Lesson 5: Where Are You From?	0.1.2, 0.2.1, 1.1.3, 5.2.3, 5.2.4	5	2.13.03
Unit 2: Giving Personal Information	**CASAS**	**LAUSD**	**Florida**
Lesson 1: The Alphabet	0.1.2, 0.1.6, 0.2.1	1, 11b, 58a, 58b	2.05.01, 2.15.02
Lesson 2: Numbers 0–9, Phone Numbers	0.1.2, 0.2.1, 6.0.1, 6.0.2	4	2.08.01
Lesson 3: Numbers 10–100, Ages	0.1.2, 0.2.1, 6.0.1, 6.0.2	3, 6	2.08.01, 2.14.01
Lesson 4: Addresses	0.1.2, 0.1.6, 0.2.1, 0.2.2	2, 7, 11	2.15.05
Lesson 5: Addressing an Envelope	2.4.1	2, 4, 8	
Lesson 6: Personal Information Forms	0.2.2	4, 6, 7, 9c	2.15.05

*CASAS: Comprehensive Adult Student Assessment System
**LAUSD: Los Angeles Unified School District (ESL Beginning Low content standards)
***Florida: Adult ESOL Low Beginning Standardized Syllabi

Unit 3: Going to School	CASAS	LAUSD	Florida
Lesson 1: The Classroom	0.1.5	11, 15, 18	
Lesson 2: Places at School	0.1.2	9d, 17	
Lesson 3: Ordinal Numbers 1st–10th	0.1.2	17	2.08.01
Lesson 4: Ordinal Numbers 11th–99th	N/A		2.08.01
Lesson 5: People at School	0.1.2	1, 16, 17	

Unit 4: Time, Dates, and Weather	CASAS	LAUSD	Florida
Lesson 1: Time	0.1.2, 2.3.1	25	
Lesson 2: Days of the Week	0.1.2, 2.3.2	26	2.08.03
Lesson 3: Months and Seasons of the Year	0.1.2, 2.3.2	26, 28	2.08.03
Lesson 4: Dates	0.1.2, 2.3.2	3, 26	2.08.03
Lesson 5: National Holidays	0.1.2, 2.3.2, 2.7.1	26, 40	2.08.03
Lesson 6: Famous Americans	5.2.1	41	
Lesson 7: Weather	0.1.2, 1.1.5, 2.3.3	28, 29	2.13.01

Unit 5: Food Unit 5: Community	CASAS	LAUSD	Florida
Lesson 1: Places in Town	0.1.2, 1.1.3, 2.2.1, 2.5.1, 2.5.3, 2.5.5	9d, 22, 23b	
Lesson 2: Transportation	0.1.2, 2.2.3	13, 24	2.09.01
Lesson 3: Transportation Routes	0.1.2, 2.2.2, 2.2.3	9d, 24a, 24b	2.05.01
Lesson 4: Transportation Schedules	0.1.2, 2.2.4		
Lesson 5: Traffic Signs	1.9.1	42	2.09.01

Unit 6: Money and Shopping	CASAS	LAUSD	Florida
Lesson 1: Money	0.1.2, 1.1.6, 6.0.2	9d, 30a	2.08.04
Lesson 2: Receipts	1.3.3, 1.6.4, 6.1.2, 6.2.2	30b	2.11.01, 2.11.03
Lesson 3: Clothing	0.1.2, 1.3.9	33	
Lesson 4: Sizes	0.1.2, 1.1.9, 1.3.9	34	2.05.01, 2.11.04
Lesson 5: Prices	0.1.2, 1.1.6, 1.2.1, 1.3.9	31	2.11.01
Lesson 6: Shopping	0.1.2, 1.3.9	9d, 32	2.05.01
Unit 7: Food	CASAS	LAUSD	Florida
Lesson 1: Food	0.1.2, 1.3.8	14a, 35	2.05.03, 2.07.09
Lesson 2: Food Containers	1.1.7, 1.3.8		2.07.09
Lesson 3: Food Quantities and Prices	0.1.2, 1.1.4, 1.1.7, 1.2.1, 1.3.8	31, 36	2.11.01, 2.11.02
Lesson 4: At a Restaurant	1.3.8, 2.6.4	35, 37	2.07.09, 2.07.11
Unit 8: Housing	CASAS	LAUSD	Florida
Lesson 1: Home	0.1.2, 1.4.1	38	
Lesson 2: Furniture and Appliances	0.1.2, 1.4.1	38	
Lesson 3: Life at Home	0.1.2, 0.2.4	12	2.05.01
Lesson 4: Reading Housing Ads	0.1.2, 1.4.2	39	2.11.06, 2.11.08
Unit 9: Talking on the Phone	CASAS	LAUSD	Florida
Lesson 1: Making Personal Calls	2.1.7, 2.1.8	19, 20	2.05.01, 2.06.02
Lesson 2: Making Business Calls	2.1.7, 2.1.8	19, 20	2.05.01, 2.06.02
Lesson 3: Calling In to Work	0.1.2, 4.4.1	57	2.02.01

Unit 10: Health	CASAS	LAUSD	Florida
Lesson 1: Parts of the Body	3.1.1	43	
Lesson 2: Feeling Sick	0.1.4, 3.1.1	44	2.05.01, 2.07.01, 2.07.02
Lesson 3: An Appointment with the Doctor	2.3.2, 3.1.2	11, 27	2.07.04, 2.08.03
Lesson 4: A Visit to the Doctor's Office	3.1.1	46	2.07.05
Unit 11: Safety Procedures	**CASAS**	**LAUSD**	**Florida**
Lesson 1: Safety Signs	0.1.3, 3.4.1, 4.3.1	49	2.10.01, 2.10.03
Lesson 2: Safety Warnings	0.1.3, 3.4.2	48	2.02.03
Lesson 3: Fire Safety at School or Work	0.1.3, 3.4.2	47	2.10.02
Lesson 4: Earthquake Safety	0.1.3, 3.4.2	47	2.10.02
Lesson 5: Call 911	0.1.2, 2.1.2, 2.5.1	21	2.06.05, 2.10.02
Unit 12: Employment	**CASAS**	**LAUSD**	**Florida**
Lesson 1: Occupations I	0.1.2, 4.1.8	50	2.01.01
Lesson 2: Occupations II	0.1.2, 4.1.8	51	2.01.01
Lesson 3: Looking for a Job	4.1.2, 4.1.3, 4.1.6	52, 53	2.01.02, 2.01.07
Lesson 4: A Job Interview	0.1.2, 0.1.3, 4.1.5, 4.1.6, 4.1.7, 4.1.8	14b, 54	2.01.04
Lesson 5: Work Schedules	0.1.2, 4.4.3	55	2.02.04, 2.08.03
Lesson 6: Reporting Problems on the Job	.5.1, 4.5.7, 4.6.4	56a, 56b	2.02.02, 2.03.03, 2.04.01

To the Teacher

Course Overview

Life Skills and Test Prep 1 is a competency-based, four-skills course for adult ESL students at the low-beginning level. It is designed to help students acquire the language and life skills competencies they need in all their roles—at home, at work, in school, and in their communities. The course also includes listening and reading tests to give students invaluable practice in taking standardized tests, motivating them to achieve their benchmarks and persist in their learning goals.

Unit Organization

There are twelve units, organized thematically. Each unit contains from three to seven lessons, each one focusing on a specific competency, such as ordering in a restaurant, identifying rooms of a house, or following a doctor's instructions. The first page of the unit lists the lessons in the unit, along with the goal for each lesson.

At the end of each unit, there is a unit test with both a listening and a reading section. This unit test is a multiple-choice test, much like the CASAS test or other standardized tests. Students must bubble in their answers on a separate answer sheet, found in the back of the book. The answer sheet is perforated so students can easily remove it.

Lesson Organization

Lessons are composed of the following elements as appropriate for the competency being presented:

- Learn
- Practice
- Make It Yours
- Listen
- Note
- Bonus

1 *Note:* Listening activities occur throughout the lesson. The icon before the direction line indicates the CD number and track.

Learn

Each lesson begins with a section called Learn, where the target competency is introduced. Some competencies focus on speaking and listening, while others focus on reading and writing. However, all four skills are integrated within the lesson.

Practice

In the Practice section, students apply what they have just learned. Practice exercises vary in type, depending on the competency. Practice sections often present model conversations, such as a server taking a customer's food order. Here are the steps for most model conversations:

1. Students first listen to the conversation.
2. They listen and repeat.
3. They practice the conversation in pairs.
4. They reverse roles and practice the conversation again.
5. They practice the conversation again, substituting other information provided.

Make It Yours

This section allows students to personalize the material. These activities range from controlled role plays to more open-ended discussions.

Note: In some activities, students may wish to use made-up information to protect their privacy.

Listen

In addition to the listening exercises built into the other sections of the lesson, every unit includes at least one Listen section that focuses on listening discrimination. The Listen section further reinforces the material in the lesson.

Note

Notes on language and culture appear in the lesson as needed. Additional notes give practical information related to the life skill competency. For example, a note in a lesson about calling 911 explains that 911 is only for emergencies. For all other situations, students should call the police department.

Bonus

The Bonus section that occurs at the end of lessons presents optional activities that go beyond the competency, giving students additional speaking and writing practice.

Unit Tests

Unit tests appear after every unit and contain both a listening and a reading section.

Listening

The listening section includes a variety of item types and is divided into two parts: Listening I and Listening II.

In Listening I, students listen to the questions but read the answer choices on the test page. The directions for this section are as follows:

- Look at the pictures and listen. What is the correct answer: A, B, or C?

In Listening II, everything—all questions and answers—is on the audio CD. The answer choices are *not* on the test page. The directions for this section are as follows:

- Listen. Everything is on the audio CD. Listen to the question and three answers. What is the correct answer: A, B, or C?

Each question in the listening sections is on a separate track on the audio CD. We recommend that you *play each track twice*, pausing for 10 to 20 seconds between each play. This will approximate how listening is presented on standardized tests.

Reading

The reading section tests students' ability to read and answer questions about a variety of print material, such as receipts, ads, phone messages, and schedules.

Answer Sheets

Each unit test is formatted like a standardized test. Students fill in (bubble in) their answers on the perforated answer sheets included in the back of the book. The answer sheets are printed on both sides of the page in case you want the students to take a test twice or to have additional practice completing the required personal information.

Answer Keys

The answer keys and audioscripts for the tests are found in the *Life Skills and Test Prep 1 Teacher's Manual*. Each answer key can be used as a scoring mask to make tests easy to grade. It also serves as a diagnostic tool; each test item is labeled with its corresponding objective, giving you a clear picture of which competencies the student has not yet acquired.

Life Skills and Test Prep 1 Teacher's Manual

In addition to the answer keys described above, the *Life Skills and Test Prep 1 Teacher's Manual* includes a section to prepare students for the tests in the book and for standardized tests. It helps students use an answer sheet, understand the directions in a test, and learn important test-taking strategies. We recommend that you go through this section of the manual with students before they take the Unit 1 test or before they take the post-test on a standardized test.

The manual also includes a Classroom Methodology section, with general information for using the *Life Skills and Test Prep 1* material. This section suggests ways for doing pair and group work activities, presenting vocabulary, checking answers, and correcting students' language production.

Please ask your Pearson Longman rep about this manual if you do not already have it.

Built-in Flexibility

Life Skills and Test Prep 1 provides 80 to 100 hours of class instruction. All the material in is aimed at low-beginning students. As such, the lessons do not have to be taught in a specific order, and lessons may be skipped. If you do not want to use all the lessons, here are some ideas for how to select which ones to use:

- Ask your students which topics they are interested in and teach only those lessons.
- Give the unit test as a pre-test to find out how students perform. Use the diagnostic information in the *Life Skills and Test Prep 1 Teacher's Manual* to guide you to which lessons students need.
- When using *Life Skills and Test Prep 1* along with *Center Stage 1*, use the information in the *Center Stage 1 Teacher's Edition* to direct you to specific lessons.

To the Student

Life Skills and Test Prep 1 will help you improve your scores on ESL tests like the CASAS test. It will help you prepare for these tests in several ways:

- You will learn the English skills you need for the test.

- You will learn about tests and test-taking strategies.

- You will take a test after each unit, which will give you practice in taking tests and using answer sheets.

Preparing to Take a Test

Here are some things you can do to prepare for a test.

- [ ] Get a lot of sleep the night before the test.
- [ ] Eat a meal or snack before the test.
- [ ] Bring two sharpened #2 pencils.
- [ ] Bring a pencil eraser.
- [ ] Bring a ruler or a blank piece of paper.
- [ ] Arrive early at the testing room.
- [ ] Make sure you can easily see and hear the tester.
- [ ] Turn off your cell phone.
- [ ] Try to relax and do your best! Good luck!

Unit 1 Meeting New People

Learn

A 🔘 **4** Look at the picture. Listen to the conversation. Point to the person talking.

B 🔘 **5** Listen to the conversation again. Underline the names in the sentences.

Pablo: Hello. My name is Pablo Diaz.
Su Hee: Hi. My name is Su Hee Hong.
Pablo: Nice to meet you, Su Hee.
Su Hee: Nice to meet you, too.

C 🔘 **6** Listen and repeat.

D *PAIRS.* Practice the conversation. Use your names. Take turns.

A: Hello. My name is _____.
B: Hi. My name is _____.
A: Nice to meet you, _____.
B: Nice to meet you, too.

Practice

A   Write the correct word from the box. You may need to use a capital letter.

~~hello~~	is	meet	name	nice

Pablo: ____Hello____. My _____ is Pablo Diaz.

Su Hee: Hi. My name _____ Su Hee Hong.

Pablo: Nice to _____ you, Su Hee.

Su Hee: _____ to meet you, too.

B   *PAIRS.* **Check your answers.**

Learn

Tom Kelly
First Name   Last Name

Sue Morgan
First Name   Last Name

Practice

A   Circle the correct word.

1. Tom is his   **first / last**   name.

2. Morgan is her   **first / last**   name.

B   Write.

1. Write your first name. _____

2. Write your last name. _____

Make It Yours

A   **Listen to the conversation. Listen and repeat.**

A: What's your first name?
B: My first name is Alex.
A: What's your last name?
B: My last name is Stone.

B   *PAIRS.* **Practice the conversation. Use your names. Take turns.**

Learn

A **8** **Look at the picture. Listen to the conversation. Point to the person talking.**

1. _____ 2. _____ 3. _____

 In the United States, it is polite for men and women to shake hands when they meet for the first time and when they say good-bye. People only hug or kiss friends and family.

B **9** **Listen to the conversation again. Write *Nidia*, *Martin*, and *Edwin* on the lines under the picture.**

Edwin: Nidia, this is my friend Martin. Martin, this is Nidia.
Nidia: Hi, Martin. Nice to meet you.
Martin: Nice to meet you, too.

C **10** **Listen and repeat.**

Practice

GROUPS OF 3. One student is Student A. One student is Student B. One student is Student C. Use your names. Practice the conversation. Take turns being Student A.

A: _____, this is my friend _____.

_____, this is _____.

B: Hi, _____. Nice to meet you.

C: Nice to meet you, too.

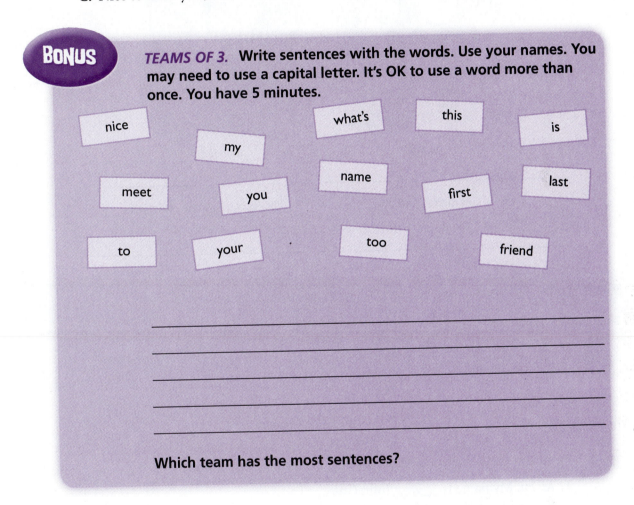

BONUS

TEAMS OF 3. Write sentences with the words. Use your names. You may need to use a capital letter. It's OK to use a word more than once. You have 5 minutes.

nice · my · what's · this · is

meet · you · name · first · last

to · your · · too · friend

_____

_____

_____

_____

_____

Which team has the most sentences?

Learn

Listen to your teacher and point. Listen and repeat.

single

married

Mr. = a man, married or single	**Mrs.** = a woman, married
Ms. = a woman, married or single	**Miss** = a woman, single

>>>>>

Use *Mr., Mrs., Ms., and Miss with last names only.*
Example:
Hello, Ms. Robinson.
Do not say Hello, Ms. Janet Robinson.
Do not say Hello, Ms. Janet.

Practice

 A   **Read the conversations. Write *Mr.* on the line or write an X.**

1. **A:** Hi. My name is ___X___ John Gold.
   B: Hello, ___Mr.___ Gold.

2. **A:** Hello, _____ Gomez.
   B: Hi, _____ Pablo.

3. **A:** Good morning, _____ Benson.
   B: Good morning, _____ Tom.

4. **A:** My name is _____ Fred Jones.
   B: Nice to meet you, _____ Jones.

B Write *Mr.*, *Ms.*, *Mrs.*, or *Miss* on the lines.

1. _____ Lee

2. _____ Thompson

3. _____ Roberts

4. _____ Sanchez

5. _____ Sanchez
   _____ Sanchez

C  **11** **Listen and check your answers.**

Make It Yours

A **Answer the questions. Use *Mr.*, *Mrs.*, *Ms.*, or *Miss*.**

1. What's your name? _____

2. What's your teacher's name? _____

3. What's a classmate's name? _____

B *PAIRS.* **Check your partner's answers.**

BONUS **What title do you use with your doctor or dentist?**

Learn

A **12** Look at the pictures. Listen and point. Listen and repeat.

daughter   father   mother   son   brother   sister

B   *PAIRS.* Student A, say a family word. Student B, point.

Practice

A   Write the words for each person on the family trees.

father   _____   _____   you

_____   you   _____   _____

B   *PAIRS.* Check your answers.

Make It Yours

A Draw a family tree for your family. Write the first names of the people in your family.

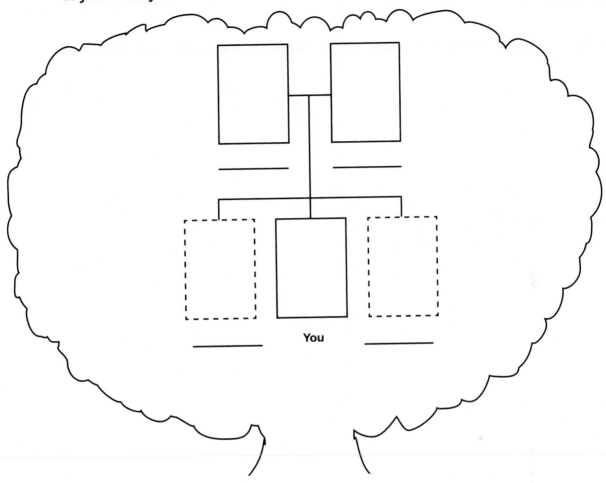

You

B *PAIRS.* Share your family tree with your partner.

Example:

A: This is my mother. My mother's name is Ana.

Listen

 13 Listen. What do you hear? Circle *a* or *b*.

1. **a.** mother   **b.** brother

2. **a.** father   **b.** daughter

3. **a.** sister   **b.** son

4. **a.** father   **b.** son

5. **a.** mother   **b.** wife

6. **a.** husband   **b.** daughter

Learn

A   **14** Look at the map of the world. Listen and point. Listen and repeat.

Canada

United States

Mexico

ATLANTIC OCEAN

PACIFIC OCEAN

Ecuador

B What other countries do you know? Show them on the map. (For the names of more countries, go to pages 196–197).

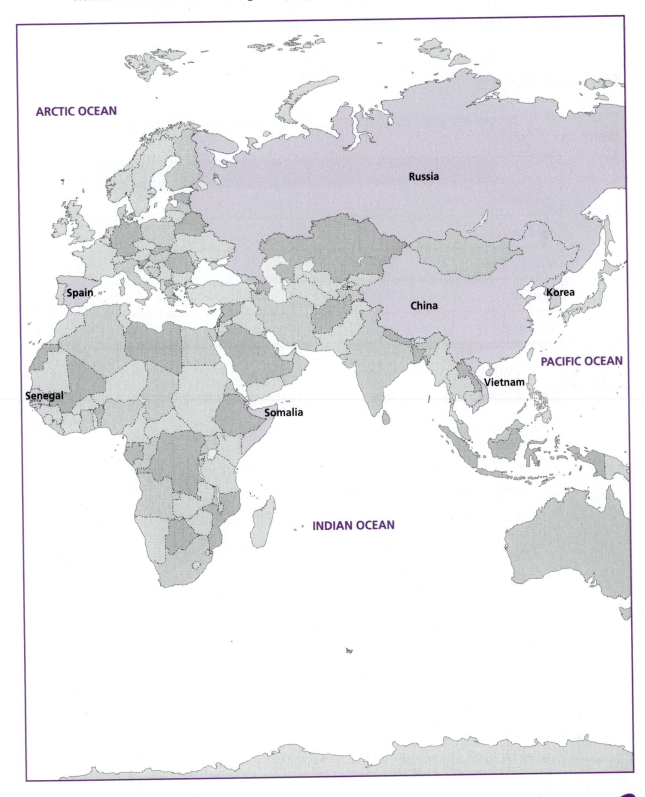

ARCTIC OCEAN

Russia

Spain

China

Korea

PACIFIC OCEAN

Senegal

Vietnam

Somalia

INDIAN OCEAN

Practice

  15 Listen to the conversation. Listen and repeat.

A: Where are you from?
B: I'm from <u>Korea</u>. How about you?
A: I'm from <u>Somalia</u>.

B *PAIRS.* Practice the conversation. Use your countries. Take turns.

Make It Yours

GROUPS OF 5. Where are you from? Ask your group. Write the countries in the chart.

	Name	Country
Student 1		
Student 2		
Student 3		
Student 4		
Student 5		

Listen

 16 Listen to the conversations. What do you hear? Circle *a*, *b*, or *c*.

1. **a.** Russia   **b.** Korea   **c.** China

2. **a.** Ecuador   **b.** Mexico   **c.** Somalia

3. **a.** Senegal   **b.** Vietnam   **c.** The United States

4. **a.** Spain   **b.** Somalia   **c.** Senegal

Learn

A   Look at the map of the United States and Canada. What state or province do you live in? Find it on the map.

B   Find the capital of your state, province, or territory. What's the name of the capital? (See the list on page 199.)

Unit 1 Test

Listening I [Tracks 17–20]

Look at the pictures and listen. What is the correct answer: A, B, or C?

1.

A

B

C

2.

A

B

C

3.

A

B

C

Listening II [Tracks 21–25]

Listen. Everything is on the audio CD.

Reading

Read. What is the correct answer: A, B, C, or D?

8. What does the woman answer?

    A. Nice to meet you, too.

    B. What's your name?

    C. My last name is Kelly.

    D. Where are you from?

9. She's Mrs. Lugo.

    A. ①

    B. ②

    C. ③

    D. ④

Unit 2 Giving Personal Information

Learn

A **26** Look at the letters. Listen and point. Listen and repeat.

Aa	**Bb**	**Cc**	**Dd**	**Ee**	**Ff**
Gg	**Hh**	**Ii**	**Jj**	**Kk**	**Ll**	**Mm**
Nn	**Oo**	**Pp**	**Qq**	**Rr**	**Ss**
Tt	**Uu**	**Vv**	**Ww**	**Xx**	**Yy**	**Zz**

B **27** *DICTATION.* Write the letters you hear.

1. _____   5. _____   9. _____

2. _____   6. _____   10. _____

3. _____   7. _____   11. _____

4. _____   8. _____   12. _____

C *PAIRS.* Check your answers.

Practice

A *PAIRS.* Student A, say a letter. Student B, say the letter after. Take turns.

> *Example:*
>
> *A:* R.
> *B:* S.
> *A: Right!*

B **28** *DICTATION.* Write the words you hear.

1. _____   3. _____   5. _____

2. _____   4. _____   6. _____

C *PAIRS.* Check your answers.

Learn

  Listen to the conversation. Listen and repeat.

Mrs. Jones: Hello. May I help you?
Mr. Ali: Hello. I'm here to see Miss Acosta.
Mrs. Jones: What's your name, please?
Mr. Ali: <u>Omar Ali</u>.
Mrs. Jones: How do you spell your first name?
Mr. Ali: It's <u>Omar</u>. <u>O-M-A-R</u>.
Mrs. Jones: And how do you spell your last name?
Mr. Ali: <u>A-L-I</u>.

Note
>>>>>
It's OK to ask people how to spell their names. It can help you remember the name.

Make It Yours

A *PAIRS.* Practice the conversation. Use your own names.

B *GROUPS OF 4.* Ask each other *What's your first name? What's your last name?* Ask *How do you spell . . .* if you need to.

Student 1 _____
First name   Last name

Student 2 _____
First name   Last name

Student 3 _____
First name   Last name

Student 4 _____
First name   Last name

BONUS **What's your middle name? Tell the class.**

Learn

A **30** Look at the numbers. Listen and point. Listen and repeat.

0	**1**	**2**	**3**	**4**	**5**	**6**	**7**	**8**	**9**
zero	one	two	three	four	five	six	seven	eight	nine

B *PAIRS.* Student A, say a number. Student B, say the number that comes before. Take turns.

> *Example:*
>
> A: 3.
> B: 2.
> A: Right!

Practice

A **31** Listen. Listen and repeat.

A: What's your phone number?
B: It's 555-1980.
A: And your area code?
B: 612.
A: Thanks.

B **32** *DICTATION.* Write the area codes and phone numbers you hear.

1. _____   3. _____   5. _____

2. _____   4. _____   6. _____

Make It Yours

PAIRS. Practice the conversation. Use your own information. (It's OK to use made-up information.)

A: What's your phone number?
B: It's _____.
A: And your area code?
B: _____.
A: Thanks.

Lesson 3 · Numbers 10–100, Ages

Learn

A **33** Look at the numbers. Listen and point. Listen and repeat.

10 ten	**17** seventeen	**24** twenty-four	**40** forty
11 eleven	**18** eighteen	**25** twenty-five	**50** fifty
12 twelve	**19** nineteen	**26** twenty-six	**60** sixty
13 thirteen	**20** twenty	**27** twenty-seven	**70** seventy
14 fourteen	**21** twenty-one	**28** twenty-eight	**80** eighty
15 fifteen	**22** twenty-two	**29** twenty-nine	**90** ninety
16 sixteen	**23** twenty-three	**30** thirty	**100** one hundred

B *PAIRS.* Student A, say a number. Student B, point. Take turns.

C *PAIRS.* Student A, say a number. Student B, write the number. Take turns.

_____ _____ _____ _____ _____ _____

Practice

> **Note**
> >>>>> Most of the time, it is not polite to ask someone's age. Sometimes we ask the ages of children or older people.

 34 Listen to the conversation. Listen and repeat.

A: Do you have any children?
B: Yes. I have a son and a daughter.
A: How old are they?
B: My son is 16. My daughter is 13.
A: That's nice.

Make It Yours

PAIRS. Practice the conversation. Use true information. If you don't have children, say, *No, I don't.*

Learn

A   **35** Look at the pictures. Listen and point. Listen and repeat.

B *PAIRS.* Student A, point to an address. Student B, say the address. Take turns.

Practice

A   **36** Listen to the conversation. Listen and repeat.

A: What's your address?
B: It's 314 Tall Oaks Road, Apartment 1.
A: That's 314 Tall Oaks Road, Apartment 1?
B: That's right.

B *PAIRS.* Practice the conversation. Use the addresses in Learn.

Learn

A Look at the compass. Listen to your teacher say the directions. Listen and point. Listen and repeat.

B *PAIRS.* Student A, say a direction. Student B, point. Take turns.

Make It Yours

PAIRS. Student A, ask Student B his or her address. Student B, answer. (It's OK to use made-up information.) Take turns.

Practice

A   **Match the words to their abbreviations.**

<u> f </u> 1. Road   a. Blvd.

_____ 2. Street   b. Apt.

_____ 3. Avenue   c. Dr.

_____ 4. Boulevard   d. St.

_____ 5. Drive   e. Ave.

_____ 6. Apartment   f. Rd.

B   **Match the words to their abbreviations.**

_____ 1. North   a. NE

_____ 2. South   b. N

_____ 3. East   c. SW

_____ 4. Northeast   d. S

_____ 5. West   e. W

_____ 6. Southwest   f. E

C   *PAIRS.* **Check your answers.**

Make It Yours

Complete the form. (It's OK to use made-up information.) For state postal abbreviations, see page 199.

Name _____
Street Address _____ Apt. # _____
City _____ State _____ Zip Code _____

Listen

37   **Listen. What do you hear? Circle *a* or *b*.**

1.   **a.** 9516 N. Beach Ave.   **b.** 9516 S. Beach Ave.

2.   **a.** 227 E. New York St.   **b.** 227 W. New York St.

3.   **a.** 320 Tall Oaks Rd.   **b.** 320 Tall Oaks Dr.

4.   **a.** 1306 Hudson Blvd.   **b.** 3006 Hudson Blvd.

5.   **a.** 185 Park Ave. NE   **b.** 185 Park Ave. NW

Addressing an Envelope

Learn

A Listen to your teacher say the parts of the envelope. Listen and repeat.

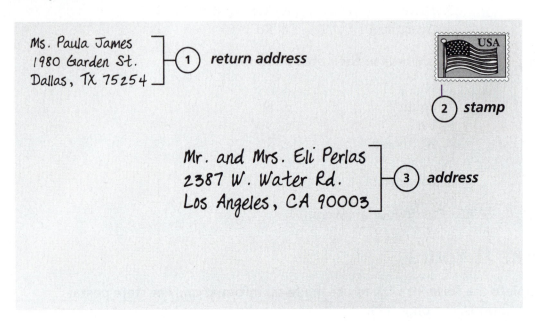

B Look at the envelope again. Answer the questions. Circle *a* or *b*.

1. Who is sending the letter?

   a. Paula James   b. Mr. and Mrs. Perlas

2. Who is getting the letter?

   a. Paula James   b. Mr. and Mrs. Perlas

3. Where is the letter going?

   a. Dallas   b. Los Angeles

4. What state is in the return address?

   a. Texas   b. California

5. What is 90003?

   a. the area code   b. the zip code

Practice

Dana Clark's address is 213 Maple Street in Orlando, Florida. Her zip code is 32819. She is sending a letter to Ms. Claire Costas. Ms. Costas's address is 2133 Park Avenue, Apartment 14A, in New York, New York. Her zip code is 10016.

 A   Address the envelope.

 B   *PAIRS.* Check your answers.

Make It Yours

Address an envelope to a friend or family member or to your teacher at the school address. Remember to write your return address.

BONUS   *PAIRS.* **Why is it important to write your return address?**

Learn

A   **38** Look at the form. Listen and point. Listen and repeat.

DIRECTIONS: Please print clearly. Use blue or black ink.

1. TITLE: Mr. (Mrs.) Miss Ms.

2. NAME: ___**Kim**___ ___**N**___ ___**Phan**___
   FIRST NAME   MIDDLE INITIAL   LAST NAME

3. ADDRESS: ___**231 Maple Street**___ ___**2E**___
   NUMBER AND STREET   APARTMENT
   ___**Los Angeles**___ ___**CA**___ ___**90006**___
   CITY   STATE   ZIP CODE

4. TELEPHONE: ___**213-555-5444**___ ___**213-555-7777**___
   HOME   OTHER

5. SEX: MALE _____ FEMALE __**X**__

6. MARITAL STATUS:
   MARRIED __**X**__ SINGLE _____ DIVORCED _____ SEPARATED _____

7. SOCIAL SECURITY NUMBER (SSN): ___**123-45-6789**___

8. SIGNATURE: ___*Kim N. Phan*___

B Read the form. Read the sentences. Circle *T* for *True* or *F* for *False*.

1. The person's name is Mrs. Phan N. Kim.   T   F

2. She lives at 231 Maple Avenue.   T   F

3. She lives in an apartment.   T   F

4. She lives in Los Alamos.   T   F

5. She has two phone numbers.   T   F

C *PAIRS.* Check your answers.

Make It Yours

Complete the form. (It's OK to use made-up information.)

DIRECTIONS: Please print clearly. Use blue or black ink.

1. TITLE: Mr.   Mrs.   Miss   Ms.

2. NAME: _____
                 FIRST NAME   MIDDLE INITIAL   LAST NAME

3. ADDRESS: _____
                   NUMBER AND STREET   APARTMENT

                _____
                     CITY   STATE   ZIP CODE

4. TELEPHONE: _____
                    HOME   OTHER

5. SEX: MALE _____   FEMALE _____

6. MARITAL STATUS:
  MARRIED _____   SINGLE _____   DIVORCED _____   SEPARATED _____

7. SOCIAL SECURITY NUMBER (SSN): _____

8. SIGNATURE: _____

Note >>>>>   *Be careful! Keep your personal information private.*

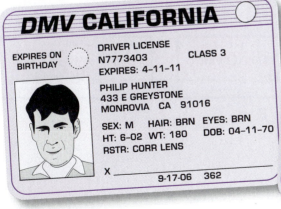

Unit 2 Test

Before you take the test

Ⓐ Ⓑ Ⓒ Ⓓ | Use the answer sheet for Unit 2 on page 207.

1. Print your name.
2. Print your teacher's name.
3. Write your student identification number, and bubble in the information below the boxes.
4. Write the test date and bubble in the information.
5. Write your class number and bubble in the information.

Listening I [Tracks 39–42]

Look at the pictures and listen. What is the correct answer: A, B, or C?

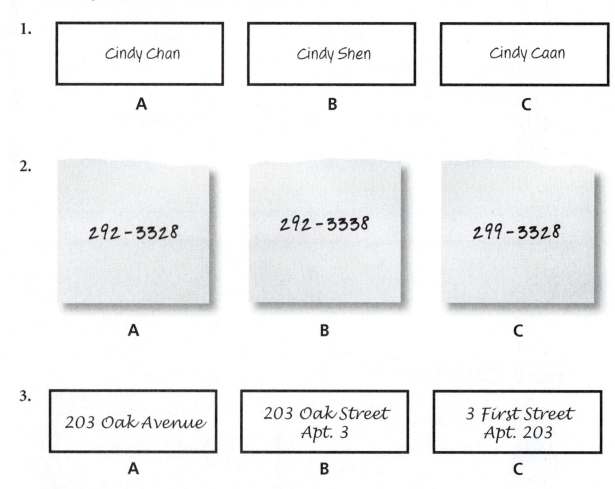

1.

Cindy Chan	Cindy Shen	Cindy Caan
A	**B**	**C**

2.

292-3328	292-3338	299-3328
A	**B**	**C**

3.

203 Oak Avenue	203 Oak Street Apt. 3	3 First Street Apt. 203
A	**B**	**C**

Listening II [Tracks 43–45]

Listen. Everything is on the audio CD.

Reading

Read. What is the correct answer: A, B, C, or D?

6. Fill in the blank.

    A. m

    B. M

    C. O

    D. n

7. What does the woman answer?

    A. 9

    B. 909

    C. 1983

    D. 996-7321

Mr. Juan Fuentes
546 Plum St.
Cocoa, FL 32926

Ms. Marie Laporte
1436 Lexington Ave., Apt. 202
New York, NY 10128

8. Who is sending the letter?

    A. Florida

    B. Marie Laporte

    C. Juan Fuentes

    D. New York

9. What is Ms. Laporte's apartment number?

    A. 546

    B. 10128

    C. 202

    D. 1436

DIRECTIONS: Please print clearly. Use blue or black ink.

NAME _____ Kyung-a _____ Son _____
FIRST NAME   MIDDLE INITIAL   LAST NAME

ADDRESS _____ 23 W. Gorham St. _____
                        NUMBER AND STREET   APARTMENT

_____ Madison _____ WI _____ 53704 _____
                        CITY   STATE   ZIP CODE

TELEPHONE _____ 608-555-5444 _____
                           HOME   OTHER

MARITAL STATUS
        MARRIED __X__ SINGLE _____ DIVORCED _____ SEPARATED _____

SOCIAL SECURITY NUMBER (SSN) __123-45-6789__

DATE OF BIRTH (DOB) _____7/13/70_____
                        MONTH/DAY/YEAR

SIGNATURE ___*Kyung-a Son*___ DATE ___4/12/07___

---

10. What is the person's last name?

    A. Kyung-a

    B. Son

    C. Gorham

    D. Madison

11. What is the person's marital status?

    A. married

    B. single

    C. divorced

    D. separated

Unit 3 Going to School

Learn

A **46** Look at the picture. Listen and point. Listen and repeat.

1. board	5. window	9. table	13. book
2. map	6. pencil	10. chair	14. paper
3. door	7. notebook	11. desk	15. pen
4. clock	8. computer	12. dictionary	16. bookcase

B   *PAIRS.* **Student A, say a word. Student B, point. Take turns.**

Practice

A   Listen to your teacher. Listen and repeat.

A: How do you say this in English?
B: <u>Door</u>.

B   *PAIRS.* **Practice the conversation. Use the objects in Learn.**

C Look at the pictures. Cover the words in Learn and label the objects.

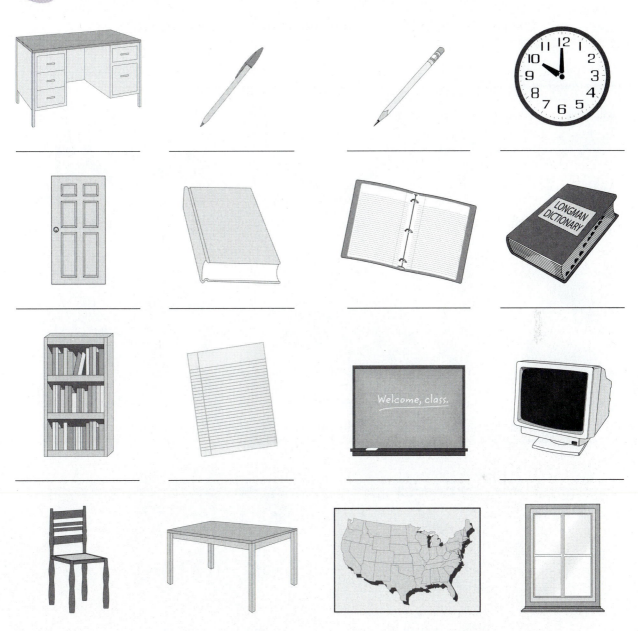

_____   _____   _____   _____

_____   _____   _____   _____

_____   _____   _____   _____

_____   _____   _____   _____

Make It Yours

PAIRS. Student A, say a word. Student B, point to the object in your classroom. Take turns.

Learn

A **47** **Look at the pictures. Listen and point. Listen and repeat.**

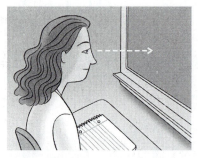

___ Look at the board.

___ Open your book.

___ Close your book.

___ Raise your hand.

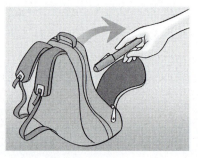

___ Take out a pen.

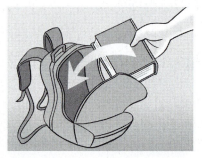

___ Put away your dictionary.

___ Write in your notebook.

___ Copy the sentence.

B  **48** **Listen. Number the pictures in the order you hear them.**

Practice

A   Complete the sentences. Match the words.

1. Take out __b__   a. your hand.

2. Write on ___   b. a pen.

3. Close ___   c. the board.

4. Raise ___   d. your book.

5. Copy ___   e. your pencil.

6. Put away ___   f. the word.

B   **49** Listen and check your answers.

Make It Yours

PAIRS.   **Student A, give an instruction. Student B, do it. Take turns.**

Example:

A: *Look at the board.*

B:

BONUS   *TEAMS OF 3.* **Use these sentence starters to write as many sentences as you can. You have 5 minutes.**

1. Take out _____.

2. Put away _____.

3. Open _____.

4. Close _____.

5. Write _____.

Which team has the most sentences?

Learn

A   CD 1 TRACK **50**   **Look at the picture. Listen and point. Listen and repeat.**

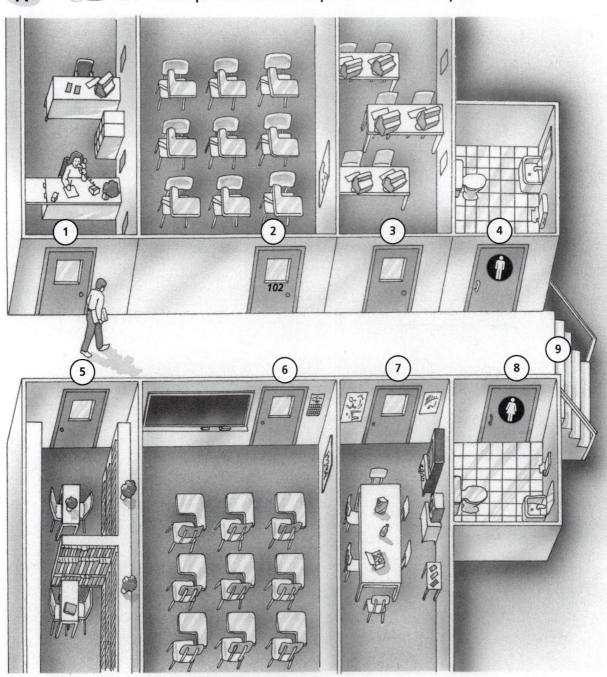

102

1. office	4. men's room	7. student lounge
2. classroom	5. library	8. ladies' room
3. computer lab	6. classroom	9. stairs

B **Look at the picture of the school on page 38. Complete the sentences. Use *across from* and *next to*.**

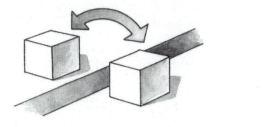

across from

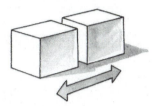

next to

1. The library is _____ the office.

2. The office is _____ Room 102.

3. The computer lab is _____ the student lounge.

4. The men's room is _____ the computer lab.

5. The ladies' room is _____ the men's room.

6. The stairs are _____ the ladies' room.

C 🔘 **51** **Listen and check your answers. Listen and repeat.**

D **Write two sentences. Use *across from* or *next to*.**

1. Room 102 _____.

2. The student lounge _____.

E *PAIRS.* **Check your answers.**

Practice

A 🔘 **52** **Listen to the conversation. Listen and repeat.**

A: Excuse me. Where's the <u>library</u>?
B: The <u>library</u>? The <u>library</u> is <u>across from</u> the <u>office</u>.
A: Thank you.

B *PAIRS.* **Practice the conversation. Use other places from Learn. Take turns.**

Make It Yours

A   Draw a map of your school. Include the office, the computer lab, the library, the student lounge, the men's room, the ladies' room, and classrooms. Write the names of the rooms on your map.

B   Write five sentences about your map.

> *Example:*
> _____ The office is next to the library. _____

1. _____.
2. _____.
3. _____.
4. _____.
5. _____.

C   *PAIRS.* Share your map and sentences.

BONUS   *PAIRS.* Student A, ask for the location of a place in your school. Student B, say where it is next to or across from. Take turns.

Example:

A: *Excuse me. Where's the computer lab?*
B: *It's next to the student lounge.*
A: *Thanks.*

Learn

A CD1 TRACK 53 **Look at the ordinal numbers. Listen and point. Listen and repeat.**

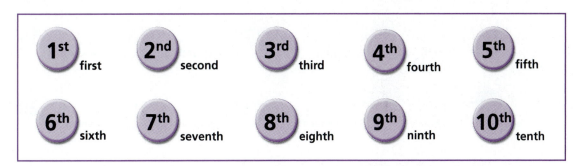

1ˢᵗ first	2ⁿᵈ second	3ʳᵈ third	4ᵗʰ fourth	5ᵗʰ fifth
6ᵗʰ sixth	7ᵗʰ seventh	8ᵗʰ eighth	9ᵗʰ ninth	10ᵗʰ tenth

B *PAIRS.* **Student A, say an ordinal number. Student B, point. Take turns.**

Practice

A **Listen to your teacher. Listen and repeat.**

A: Where is Room 204?
B: It's on the second floor.

B *PAIRS.* **Student A, ask where a room is. Student B, say what floor it's on. Take turns.**

Room 325	Room 817
Room 503	Room 947
Room 1050	Room 798

Note >>>>> *The first floor is also called the ground floor or the lobby.*

Make It Yours

PAIRS. **Student A, ask where a place is in your school. Student B, say what floor it's on. Take turns.**

Example:
A: Where is the office?
B: It's on the first floor.

Learn

A Look at the ordinal numbers. Listen and point. Listen and repeat.

11th eleventh   **12th** twelfth   **13th** thirteenth   **14th** fourteenth   **15th** fifteenth

16th sixteenth   **17th** seventeenth   **18th** eighteenth   **19th** nineteenth   **20th** twentieth

21st twenty-first   **22nd** twenth-second   **23rd** twenty-third   **30th** thirtieth   **40th** fortieth

50th fiftieth   **60th** sixtieth   **70th** seventieth   **80th** eightieth   **90th** ninetieth

B   *PAIRS.* Student A, say an ordinal number. Student B, write it. Take turns.

Listen

 Listen. What do you hear? Circle *a*, *b*, or *c*.

1.   **a.** 51st   **b.** 15th   **c.** 50th
2.   **a.** 17th   **b.** 73rd   **c.** 77th
3.   **a.** 45th   **b.** 40th   **c.** 44th
4.   **a.** 22nd   **b.** 33rd   **c.** 63rd
5.   **a.** 88th   **b.** 80th   **c.** 82nd
6.   **a.** 39th   **b.** 19th   **c.** 91st

BONUS   Do any streets in your neighborhood use ordinal numbers?

3rd Ave.   11th St.

Learn

 56 Look at the pictures. Listen and point. Listen and repeat.

1. ____principal____

2. _____

3. _____

4. _____

5. _____

6. _____

Practice

A Write the words under the correct pictures.

custodian	receptionist	student
~~principal~~	security guard	teacher

B *PAIRS.* Check your answers.

> **Example:**
> A: Who's this?
> B: The <u>principal</u>.

Make It Yours

PAIRS. Answer the questions.

1. What's your principal's or director's name? _____

2. Where is his or her office? _____

Unit 3 Test

 Listening I [Tracks 57–61]

Look at the pictures and listen. What is the correct answer: A, B, or C?

1.

A B C

2.

A B C

3.

A B C

4.

5ᵗʰ *Floor*	15ᵗʰ *Floor*	50ᵗʰ *Floor*
A	B	C

 Listening II [Tracks 62–64]

Listen. Everything is on the audio CD.

44 Unit 3 Test

Reading

Read. What is the correct answer: A, B, C, or D?

7. What is this?

   A. a desk

   B. a dictionary

   C. a board

   D. a clock

8. What is the teacher's instruction?

      A. Put away your dictionary.

      B. Please look at the board.

      C. Please open your book.

      D. Please take out a pen.

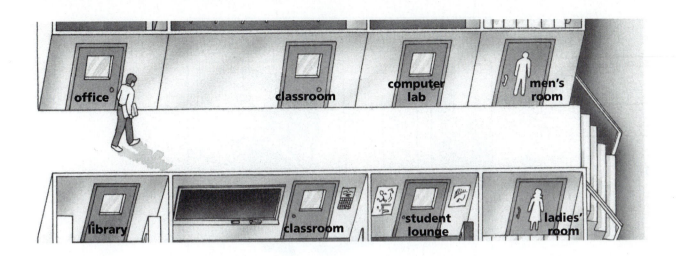

9. Where is the student lounge?

    A. next to the computer lab

    B. across from the computer lab

    C. next to the office

    D. across from the library

10. What does Mr. Green do?

 A. He's a custodian.

 B. He's a teacher.

 C. He's a student.

 D. He's a principal.

Unit 4 Time, Dates, and Weather

Lesson 1 **Time**
- Read the time and ask for the time

Lesson 2 **Days of the Week**
- Identify and spell the days of the week

Lesson 3 **Months and Seasons of the Year**
- Use the months of the year and their abbreviations
- Use the seasons of the year

Lesson 4 **Dates**
- Read, write, and say the dates

Lesson 5 **National Holidays**
- Recognize dates of major holidays

Lesson 6 **Famous Americans**
- Learn about Dr. Martin Luther King, Jr., President George Washington, and President Abraham Lincoln

Lesson 7 **Weather**
- Talk about the weather

Learn

A 🔘 CD2 TRACK 2 Look at the clocks. Listen and point. Listen and repeat.

1:00	2:05	3:10	4:15
5:20	6:25	7:30	8:35
9:40	10:45	11:50	12:55

Note
>>>>>

We say, "It's five twenty."   5:20

B   *PAIRS.* Student A, point to a clock. Student B, say the time. Take turns.

Practice

A   Listen to your teacher. Listen and repeat.

A: What time is it?
B: It's 1:00.

B   *PAIRS.* Practice the conversation. Use other times in Learn. Then use the real time.

Learn

Listen to your teacher. Listen and repeat.

A.M. = in the morning   P.M. = { in the afternoon
in the evening
at night

Practice

Write the time expression on the line.

1. 11:15 A.M.   11:15 _in the morning_____
2. 4:10 P.M.   4:10 _____
3. 7:50 P.M.   7:50 _____
4. 10:25 P.M.   10:25 _____

Make It Yours

Fill in the chart for three classmates. Write their names.

What time do you have breakfast?			
What time do you have lunch?			
What time do you have dinner?			

Listen

3 **Listen to the conversations. What do you hear? Circle *a*, *b*, or *c*.**

1. a.  b.   c.

2. a.   b.   c.

3. a.   b.   c.

4. a.  b.  c.

BONUS   What time is midnight? _____

What time is noon? _____

Learn

A **4** **Look at the calendar. Listen and point. Listen and repeat.**

			OCTOBER			
Sunday	Monday	Tuesday	Wednesday	Thursday	Friday	Saturday
1	2	3	4	5	6	7

B   *PAIRS.* **Student A, say a day. Student B, point. Take turns.**

C   *PAIRS.* **Student A, say a day. Student B, say the day after. Take turns.**

> *Example:*
> A: *Sunday*
> B: *Monday*

Practice

A   **Listen to your teacher. Listen and repeat.**

A: What day is today?
B: It's <u>Monday</u>.

B   *PAIRS.* **What day is today? Ask your partner.**

Learn

A   **Match the days to their abbreviations.**

<u>g</u> 1. Sunday   a. Thurs.

___ 2. Monday   b. Tues.

___ 3. Tuesday   c. Sat.

___ 4. Wednesday   d. Mon.

___ 5. Thursday   e. Fri.

___ 6. Friday   f. Wed.

___ 7. Saturday   g. Sun.

B   *PAIRS.* **Check your answers.**

C Cover Exercise A in Learn. Write the missing days. Use abbreviations.

Sun.						
1	2	3	4	5	6	7

Practice

A Look at the class schedule. Practice the conversation.

A: When is <u>ESL 1</u>?
B: It's on <u>Monday, Wednesday, and Friday</u>.

	Mon.	Tues.	Wed.	Thurs.	Fri.
ESL 1	X		X		X
ESL 2		X		X	X
ESL 3		X		X	

B *PAIRS.* Practice the conversation. Use other classes in the schedule.

Listen

5 Listen. What do you hear? Circle the day or days you hear.

1. Sun. Mon. Tues. Wed. Thurs. Fri. Sat.

2. Sun. Mon. Tues. Wed. Thurs. Fri. Sat.

3. Sun. Mon. Tues. Wed. Thurs. Fri. Sat.

BONUS Answer the questions.

1. What days are the weekend? _____ and _____

2. What are other abbreviations for the days of the week? (Hint: See page 54.)

   Sunday _____   Thursday _____

   Monday _____   Friday _____

   Tuesday _____   Saturday _____

   Wednesday _____

Lesson 3 **Months and Seasons of the Year**

Learn

A 🎵 CD2 TRACK 6 **Look at the calendar. Listen and point. Listen and repeat.**

JANUARY	FEBRUARY	MARCH	APRIL
S M T W T F S	S M T W T F S	S M T W T F S	S M T W T F S
1 2 3 4 5 6	1 2 3	1 2 3	1 2 3 4 5 6 7
7 8 9 10 11 12 13	4 5 6 7 8 9 10	4 5 6 7 8 9 10	8 9 10 11 12 13 14
14 15 16 17 18 19 20	11 12 13 14 15 16 17	11 12 13 14 15 16 17	15 16 17 18 19 20 21
21 22 23 24 25 26 27	18 19 20 21 22 23 24	18 19 20 21 22 23 24	22 23 24 25 26 27 28
28 29 30 31	25 26 27 28	25 26 27 28 29 30 31	29 30

MAY	JUNE	JULY	AUGUST
S M T W T F S	S M T W T F S	S M T W T F S	S M T W T F S
1 2 3 4 5	1 2	1 2 3 4 5 6 7	1 2 3 4
6 7 8 9 10 11 12	3 4 5 6 7 8 9	8 9 10 11 12 13 14	5 6 7 8 9 10 11
13 14 15 16 17 18 19	10 11 12 13 14 15 16	15 16 17 18 19 20 21	12 13 14 15 16 17 18
20 21 22 23 24 25 26	17 18 19 20 21 22 23	22 23 24 25 26 27 28	19 20 21 22 23 24 25
27 28 29 30 31	24 25 26 27 28 29 30	29 30 31	26 27 28 29 30 31

SEPTEMBER	OCTOBER	NOVEMBER	DECEMBER
S M T W T F S	S M T W T F S	S M T W T F S	S M T W T F S
1	1 2 3 4 5 6	1 2 3	1
2 3 4 5 6 7 8	7 8 9 10 11 12 13	4 5 6 7 8 9 10	2 3 4 5 6 7 8
9 10 11 12 13 14 15	14 15 16 17 18 19 20	11 12 13 14 15 16 17	9 10 11 12 13 14 15
16 17 18 19 20 21 22	21 22 23 24 25 26 27	18 19 20 21 22 23 24	16 17 18 19 20 21 22
23 24 25 26 27 28 29	28 29 30 31	25 26 27 28 29 30	23 24 25 26 27 28 29
30			30 31

B **Listen to your teacher. Listen and repeat.**

    A: What's the <u>first</u> month?
    B: <u>January</u>.

C *PAIRS.* **Practice the conversation. Use other months. Take turns.**

> *Remember!*
> You learned ordinal numbers in Unit 3, Lessons 3 and 4.

 54 **Unit 4 Lesson 3**

Practice

A Look at the pictures. Listen to your teacher. Listen and point.
Listen and repeat.

winter   spring   summer   fall

B Write the months.

1. **Winter:** December, _____, and _____

2. **Spring:** March, _____, and _____

3. **Summer:** June, _____, and _____

4. **Fall:** _____, _____, and _____

C *PAIRS.* Check your answers.

D Look at a calendar for this year. Answer the questions.

1. What is the first day of winter? _____

2. What is the first day of spring? _____

3. What is the first day of summer? _____

4. What is the first day of fall? _____

BONUS   *PAIRS.* What's your favorite month? What's your favorite season?

Lesson 4 Dates

Learn

A CD2 TRACK 7 **Look at the calendar. Listen and point. Listen and repeat.**

			May			
Sunday	Monday	Tuesday	Wednesday	Thursday	Friday	Saturday
1	2	3	4	5	6	7
8	9	10	11	12	13	14
15	16	17	18	19	20	21
22	23	24	25	26	27	28
29	30	31				

B *PAIRS.* **Student A, say a date in May, etc. Student B, point.**

> **Note** >>>>> *We write* May 1, May 2, May 3, *etc. We say* May first, May second, May third, *etc.*

Practice

A **Listen to your teacher. Listen and repeat.**

A: What's today's date?
B: January 3. (*January third.*)

B *PAIRS.* **Practice the conversation. Use the dates in the box. Take turns.**

January 3	March 18	June 14	July 15	August 4	September 9

Make It Yours

A *PAIRS.* **What's today's date? Ask your partner.**

B *PAIRS.* **When is your birthday? Ask your partner. Take turns.**

Learn

8 Listen. Listen and point. Listen and repeat.

August 10, 2007

Receipt

March 31, 1999

2004
April 9

DECEMBER
12
2005

Practice

A **9** *DICTATION.* Write the dates you hear in words.

1. _January 15, 2005_   5. _____   9. _____
2. _____   6. _____   10. _____
3. _____   7. _____   11. _____
4. _____   8. _____   12. _____

> **Note** >>>>> *We write dates with numbers: month/day/year.*
> ***Examples:***
> *8/10/07* and *11/6/99*

B Rewrite the dates in Exercise A in numbers.

1. _1/15/05_   5. _____   9. _____
2. _____   6. _____   10. _____
3. _____   7. _____   11. _____
4. _____   8. _____   12. _____

C *PAIRS.* Check your answers.

Make It Yours

Answer the questions.

1. What is today's date? Write it in numbers and in words.

_____   _____

2. What's your date of birth (DOB)? Write it in numbers and in words.

_____   _____

Learn

A **10** **Look at the national holidays in 2006. Listen and point. Listen and repeat.**

JANUARY   2006

S	M	T	W	T	F	S
1	2	3	4	5	6	7
8	9	10	11	12	13	14
15	16	17	18	19	20	21
22	23	24	25	26	27	28
29	30	31				

January 1—New Year's Day
January 16—Martin Luther King, Jr. Day

FEBRUARY   2006

S	M	T	W	T	F	S
			1	2	3	4
5	6	7	8	9	10	11
12	13	14	15	16	17	18
19	20	21	22	23	24	25
26	27	28				

February 20—Presidents' Day

MAY   2006

S	M	T	W	T	F	S
	1	2	3	4	5	6
7	8	9	10	11	12	13
14	15	16	17	18	19	20
21	22	23	24	25	26	27
28	29	30	31			

May 29—Memorial Day

JULY   2006

S	M	T	W	T	F	S
						1
2	3	4	5	6	7	8
9	10	11	12	13	14	15
16	17	18	19	20	21	22
23	24	25	26	27	28	29
30	31					

July 4—Independence Day

SEPTEMBER   2006

S	M	T	W	T	F	S
					1	2
3	4	5	6	7	8	9
10	11	12	13	14	15	16
17	18	19	20	21	22	23
24	25	26	27	28	29	30

September 4—Labor Day

OCTOBER   2006

S	M	T	W	T	F	S
1	2	3	4	5	6	7
8	9	10	11	12	13	14
15	16	17	18	19	20	21
22	23	24	25	26	27	28
29	30	31				

October 9—Columbus Day

NOVEMBER   2006

S	M	T	W	T	F	S
			1	2	3	4
5	6	7	8	9	10	11
12	13	14	15	16	17	18
19	20	21	22	23	24	25
26	27	28	29	30		

November 11—Veterans' Day
November 23—Thanksgiving Day

DECEMBER   2006

S	M	T	W	T	F	S
					1	2
3	4	5	6	7	8	9
10	11	12	13	14	15	16
17	18	19	20	21	22	23
24	25	26	27	28	29	30
31						

December 25—Christmas Day

B *PAIRS.* **Student A, ask questions about the national holidays in 2006. Student B, answer. Take turns.**

> **Example:**
>
> A: When was <u>Presidents' Day</u>?
> B: <u>February 20.</u> (*February twentieth.*)

Learn

A   **Listen and read the information about U.S. holidays.**

> Some U.S. holidays, like Martin Luther King, Jr., Day, are always on Monday.
>
> Some U.S. holidays, like New Year's Day, are always on the same date.
>
> Two U.S. holidays are always on a certain day of the month. Labor Day, for example, is always the first Monday in September.

B *PAIRS.* **Complete the chart with the national holidays in Learn.**

Holidays that are always on Monday	Holidays that are always on the same date	Holidays that are always on a certain day of the month
Martin Luther King, Jr., Day	New Year's Day	Labor Day

Make It Yours

PAIRS. **Use a calendar for this year. Student A, ask questions about the national holidays. Student B, answer. Take turns.**

> **A:** When is <u>Veterans' Day</u>?
> **B:** <u>November 11.</u> (*November eleventh.*)

BONUS *GROUPS OF 3.* **Answer the questions.**

Do you know any other American holidays? When are they?

Learn

 12 Listen and read the information about these famous Americans.

1929–1968

Martin Luther King, Jr.
- He was the leader of the U.S. civil rights movement from the 1950s to 1968.
- He gave his famous "I have a dream" speech in 1963.
- He received the Nobel Peace Prize in 1964.
- He was assassinated on April 4, 1968.

1732–1799

President George Washington
- He was a general during the American Revolutionary War (1775–1781).
- He was the first president of the United States (1789–1797).
- He was called "The Father of Our Country."

1809–1865

President Abraham Lincoln
- He was the sixteenth president of the United States (1861–1865).
- He was president during the American Civil War (1861–1865).
- He signed the Emancipation Proclamation in 1863 to free the slaves.
- He was assassinated in 1865.

Practice

PAIRS. Student A, give a fact about one of these famous Americans. Student B, name the person. Take turns.

> *Example:*
>
> A: He received the Nobel Peace Prize in 1964.
> B: Martin Luther King, Jr.

BONUS GROUPS OF 3. **Answer the questions.**

Who is the president of the United States now? What are the names of some other U.S. presidents?

Lesson 7 — Weather

Learn

A **13** Look at the pictures. Listen and point. Listen and repeat.

_____ hot

_____ warm

_____ cool

_____ cold

_____ sunny

_____ rainy

_____ cloudy

_____ windy

_____ snowy

B **14** Listen. Number the pictures in the order you hear them.

C *PAIRS.* Check your answers.

Practice

A Listen to your teacher. Listen and repeat.

A: What's the weather like?
B: It's <u>sunny</u>.

B *PAIRS.* Practice the conversation. Use other weather words in Learn.

Make It Yours

PAIRS. What's the weather like today? Ask your partner. Take turns.

> **Example:**
> A: What's the weather like today?
> B: It's <u>sunny and warm</u>.

Note

>>>>>

90° F = ninety degrees Fahrenheit

Learn

A 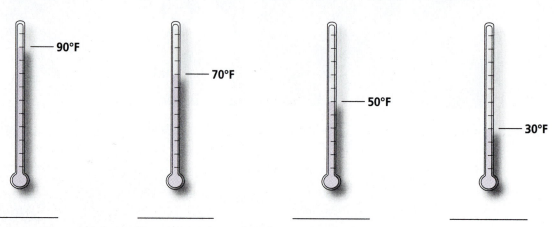 CD2 TRACK **15** **Look at the thermometers. Listen and point. Listen and repeat.**

— 90°F

— 70°F

— 50°F

— 30°F

_____   _____   _____   _____

B   **Write these words under the correct thermometer.**

cold	cool	hot	warm

Practice

A   **Listen to your teacher. Listen and repeat.**

A: What's the temperature?
B: It's <u>50°</u>. It's <u>cool</u>.

B   *PAIRS.* **Practice the conversation. Use the temperatures in the box and the weather words in Learn.**

85°	55°	72°	30°	19°

Make It Yours

PAIRS. **What's the temperature today? Ask your partner.**

Practice

16 *DICTATION.* **Listen and write.**

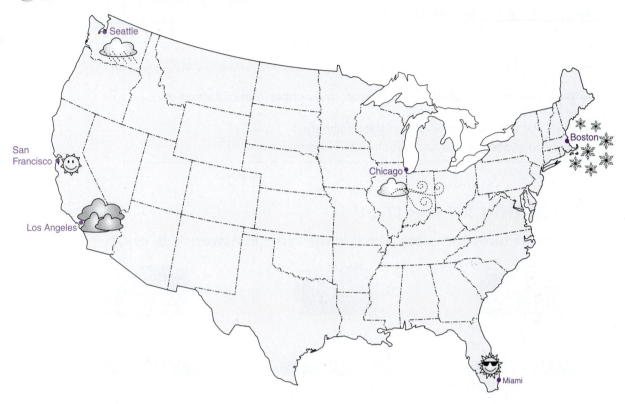

1. It's _____sunny_____ and _____cool_____ in San Francisco. It's _____60°_____.

2. It's _____ and _____ in Los Angeles. It's _____.

3. It's _____ and _____ in Seattle. It's _____.

4. It's _____ and _____ in Chicago. It's _____.

5. It's _____ and _____ in Miami. It's _____.

6. It's _____ and _____ in Boston. It's _____.

BONUS *PAIRS.* **How many seasons are there in your country? What's the weather like in each season?**

Unit 4 Test

Listening I [Tracks 17–21]

Look at the pictures and listen. What is the correct answer: A, B, or C?

1.

A   B   C

2.

JANUARY								JUNE								JULY						
S	M	T	W	T	F	S		S	M	T	W	T	F	S		S	M	T	W	T	F	S
	1	2	3	4	5	6							1	2		1	2	3	4	5	⑥	7
7	8	9	10	11	12	13		3	4	5	6	7	8	9		8	9	10	11	12	13	14
14	15	⑯	17	18	19	20		10	11	12	13	14	15	⑯		15	16	17	18	19	20	21
21	22	23	24	25	26	27		17	18	19	20	21	22	23		22	23	24	25	26	27	28
28	29	30	31					24	25	26	27	28	29	30		29	30	31				

A   B   C

3.

A   B   C

4.

JANUARY								JULY								DECEMBER						
S	M	T	W	T	F	S		S	M	T	W	T	F	S		S	M	T	W	T	F	S
	①	2	3	4	5	6		1	2	3	④	5	6	7								1
7	8	9	10	11	12	13		8	9	10	11	12	13	14		2	3	4	5	6	7	8
14	15	16	17	18	19	20		15	16	17	18	19	20	21		9	10	11	12	13	14	15
21	22	23	24	25	26	27		22	23	24	25	26	27	28		16	17	18	19	20	21	22
28	29	30	31					29	30	31						23	24	㉕	26	27	28	29
																30	31					

A   B   C

Listening II [Tracks 22–26]

Listen. Everything is on the audio CD.

Reading

Read. What is the correct answer: A, B, C, or D?

Sun.	Mon.	Tues.	Wed.	Thurs.	Fri.	Sat.
	computer class		English class	writing class		

9. When is the English class?

    A. It's on Monday.

    B. It's on Tuesday.

    C. It's on Wednesday.

    D. It's on Saturday.

DECEMBER						
S	M	T	W	T	F	S
						1
2	3	4	5	6	7	8
9	10	11	12	13	14	15
16	17	18	19	20	21	22
23	24	25	26	27	28	29
30	31					

JANUARY						
S	M	T	W	T	F	S
		1	2	3	4	5
6	7	8	9	10	11	12
13	14	15	16	17	18	19
20	21	22	23	24	25	26
27	28	29	30	31		

FEBRUARY						
S	M	T	W	T	F	S
					1	2
3	4	5	6	7	8	9
10	11	12	13	14	15	16
17	18	19	20	21	22	23
24	25	26	27	28		

10. What season is this?

    A. winter

    B. spring

    C. summer

    D. fall

```
3 / 5 / 08
```

11. What is the month?

    A. February

    B. March

    C. May

    D. August

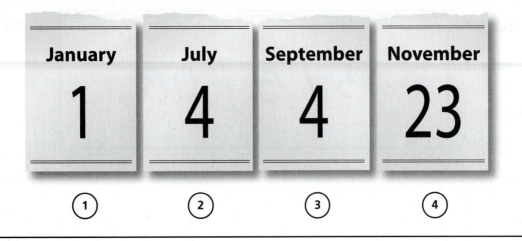

January
1
①

July
4
②

September
4
③

November
23
④

12. When is Independence Day in the United States?

    A. ①

    B. ②

    C. ③

    D. ④

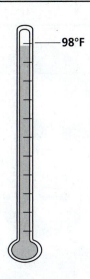

98°F

13. What is the weather like?

    A. It's cold.

    B. It's cool.

    C. It's warm.

    D. It's hot.

Abraham Lincoln

14. Who was Abraham Lincoln?

    A. the president during the American Civil War

    B. a leader of the U.S. civil rights movement

    C. the first president of the United States

    D. a winner of a Nobel Peace Prize

Unit 5 Community

Learn

A  **27** Look at the pictures. Listen and point. Listen and repeat.

library

gas station

fire station

drugstore

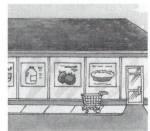

supermarket

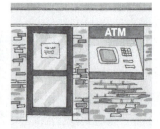

bank

post office

hospital

movie theater

B **28** Listen to five conversations. Number the pictures in the order you hear them.

a. ___

b. ___

c. ___

d. ___

e. ___

C *PAIRS.* Check your answers.

Practice

A   Listen to your teacher. Listen and repeat.

A: Where are you going?
B: I'm going to the <u>bank</u>.

B   *PAIRS.* Practice the conversation. Use other places in Learn. Take turns.

Learn

A   CD2 TRACK **29** ▶ Look at the map. Listen and point. Listen and repeat.

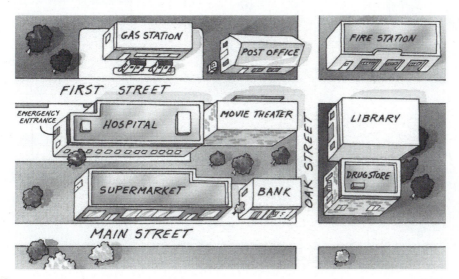

B   *PAIRS.* Student A, say a location on the map. Student B, guess the place.

> *Example:*
>
> A: It's on First Street.
> B: The gas station?
> A: No. Guess again!

Practice

A   Listen to your teacher. Listen and repeat.

A: Excuse me. Where is the <u>hospital</u>?
B: It's on <u>First Street</u>.
A: Thanks.

B   *PAIRS.* Practice the conversation. Use other places on the map.

Make It Yours

PAIRS. Ask and answer questions about places in your neighborhood.

Learn

A Write the words under the correct pictures.

bike	car	subway	van
bus	motorcycle	train	~~walk~~

1. _____walk_____

2. ride a _____

3. take the _____

4. drive a _____

5. take the _____

6. carpool in a _____

7. ride a _____

8. take the _____

B **30** Listen and check your answers. Listen and repeat.

Practice

A **31** Listen to the conversation. Listen and repeat.

A: How do you get to school?
B: I <u>drive</u>. What about you?
A: I <u>take the bus</u>.

B *PAIRS.* Practice the conversation. Use other words in Learn.

Make It Yours

A   Fill in the chart for five classmates.

Names	How do you get to work?	How do you get to school?	How do you get to the supermarket?

B   Report to the class.

> **Example:**
>
> *Anita takes the train to work. She takes the bus to school. She walks to the supermarket.*

Listen

 32   Listen to the conversations. What kind of transportation are the people talking about? Circle *a*, *b*, or *c*.

1.   **a.** subway   **b.** train   **c.** bus

2.   **a.** bike   **b.** motorcycle   **c.** bus

3.   **a.** van   **b.** car   **c.** bike

4.   **a.** train   **b.** bus   **c.** car

5.   **a.** walk   **b.** van   **c.** subway

BONUS   Take a survey. How many people in your class drive to school? Take the bus? Walk, etc.?

_____ people drive

_____ people take the bus

_____ people walk

_____ people take the subway

_____ people ride bikes

_____ people _____
                            (other)

Learn

 33 Look at the buses. Listen and point.

 15 First Street    604 City Center   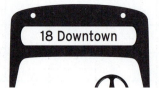 18 Downtown    10 Broadway

Practice

A   Listen to your teacher. Listen and repeat.

A: Excuse me. Which bus goes to <u>Broadway</u>?
B: The Number <u>10</u> bus.
A: The Number <u>10</u>? Thanks.
B: You're welcome.

B   *PAIRS.* Practice the conversation. Use other buses in Learn.

Learn

 34 Look at the trains. Listen and point.

 **G** Forest Hills   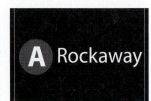 **A** Rockaway    **N** Astoria    **S** Times Square

Practice

A   Listen to your teacher. Listen and repeat.

A: Excuse me. Is this the train to <u>Rockaway</u>?
B: Yes, it is.
A: Thank you.
B: No problem.

B   *PAIRS.* Practice the conversation. Use other trains in Learn.

Learn

A   Look at the train schedule. Answer the questions.

Train 534	
To	**A.M.**
Bronxville	8:26
Mt. Vernon West	8:32
Fordham	8:43
Harlem	8:53
Grand Central	9:06

1. What time does Train 534 arrive in Bronxville? _____

2. What time does Train 534 arrive in Fordham? _____

3. What time does Train 534 arrive in Harlem? _____

4. What time does Train 534 arrive in Grand Central? _____

B   *PAIRS.* Check your answers.

Practice

PAIRS. Student A, look at this page. Student B, look at page 78.

A   Student A, ask Student B about the trains to Crestview. Write the times.

> *Example:*
> *A: What time does Train 698 arrive in Crestview?*
> *B: It arrives at 1:19 P.M.*

Train	Arrive Crestview P.M.	Arrive Springdale P.M.
698	1:19	1:25
757		2:18
832		3:26
901		4:45

B   Student A, answer Student B's questions about the trains to Springdale.

A   Student B, answer Student A's questions about the trains to Crestview.

> *Example:*
>
> A: What time does Train 698 arrive in Crestview?
> B: It arrives at 1:19 P.M.

B   Student B, ask Student A about the trains to Springdale. Write the times.

Train	Arrive Crestview P.M.	Arrive Springdale P.M.
698	1:19	1:25
757	2:05	
832	3:11	
901	4:32	

Make It Yours

PAIRS. ROLE PLAY. **Student A, you want to take the train. Student B, you're at the information desk. Student A, ask Student B for help. Take turns. Use the times in the box.**

> *Example:*
>
> A: I need to be in Center City at 9:00. What train can I take from Eastview?
> B: Take the 8:10.

8:30	9:00	9:10
10:00	9:30	9:45

Leave Eastview	Arrive Center City
7:49	8:25
8:10	8:45
8:42	9:17
8:51	9:33
9:08	9:50

BONUS

A   Is there public transportation where you live? What kind? Do you ever take it? How much does it cost?

B   Bring in a schedule for a bus or train. Go over the schedule with a group or the class.

Learn

A   Match the signs with the pictures.

a.

b.

c.

d.

e.

f.

_c_ 1. STOP

___ 2. ONE WAY

___ 3.

___ 4. NO PARKING

___ 5. R R

___ 6. DO NOT ENTER

B   CD2 TRACK 35   Look at the signs. Listen and point. Listen and repeat.

Make It Yours

Which signs do you see near your school or home? Circle the signs in Learn.

BONUS   *PAIRS.* Write the names of signs 3 and 5.

Unit 5 Test

Listening I [Tracks 36–40]

Look at the pictures and listen. What is the correct answer: A, B, or C?

1.
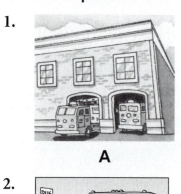

A   B   C

2.

A   B   C

3.
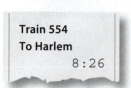

Train 554	Train 534	Train 534
To Harlem	To Harlem	To Harlem
8:26	8:26	8:56

A   B   C

4.

A   B   C

Listening II [Tracks 41–44]

Listen. Everything is on the audio CD.

Reading

Read. What is the correct answer: A, B, C, or D?

8. Where are you going?

    A. I'm going to the bank.

    B. I'm going to the drugstore.

    C. I'm going to the library.

    D. I'm going to the post office.

9. Which sentence is true?

    A. The bank is across from the supermarket.

    B. The post office is next to the bank.

    C. The post office is across from the supermarket.

    D. The supermarket is next to the bank.

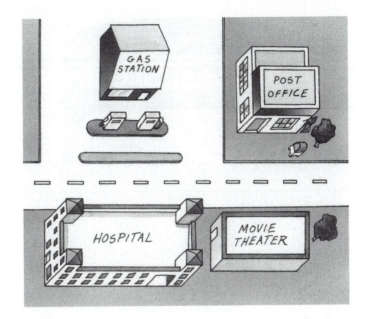

10. Where is the gas station?

    A. It's next to the hospital.

    B. It's across from the post office.

    C. It's across from the hospital.

    D. It's next to the movie theater.

11. Where does this bus go?

    A. 604th Street

    B. school

    C. 6:04 P.M.

    D. City Center

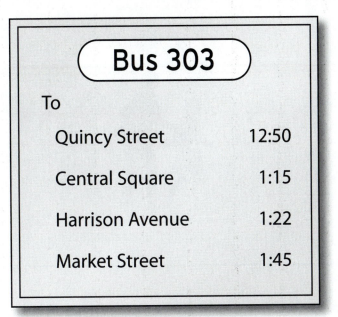

Bus 303

To

Quincy Street	12:50
Central Square	1:15
Harrison Avenue	1:22
Market Street	1:45

12. What time does Bus 303 arrive at Central Square?

A. 12:50

B. 1:15

C. 1:22

D. 1:45

13. What does this sign mean?

    A. Do not enter.

    B. This is a railroad crossing.

    C. Do not park here.

    D. This is a school crossing.

Unit 6 Money and Shopping

Learn

A **45** Look at the money. Listen and point. Listen and repeat.

1. ___$1___

2. _____

3. _____

4. _____

B *PAIRS.* Write the amounts under the correct bills.

$5	$20	$1	$10

C *PAIRS.* Student A, say an amount. Student B, point to the bill. Take turns.

D *PAIRS.* Match the pictures of the coins and their names.

a.

b.

c.

d.

_b_ 1. a nickel

___ 2. a dime

___ 3. a quarter

___ 4. a penny

E **46** Listen and check your answers. Listen and repeat.

F *PAIRS.* **Write the amounts in words.**

1. A penny is _____*one*_____ cent.

2. A nickel is _____ cents.

3. A dime is _____ cents.

4. A quarter is _____ cents.

G *PAIRS.* **Look at the coins. Fill in the numbers.**

1. $1.00 = _____ quarters

2. $1.00 = _____ quarters and _____ dimes

3. $1.00 = _____ quarter, _____ dimes, and _____ nickels

Practice

A Listen to your teacher. Listen and repeat.

A: Excuse me. Do you have change for a dollar?
B: Yes. I have <u>four quarters</u>.
A: Thanks.

B *PAIRS.* Practice the conversation. Use other amounts of money. (Hint: See Exercise G on page 89.)

Learn

A CD2 TRACK 47 Look at the amounts. Listen and point. Listen and repeat.

$2.99	$43.25	$58.00	$79.03	$110.50

B Write the amount in numbers.

1. twenty-five dollars and sixty-five cents $25.65

2. fifteen dollars and eighty-two cents _____

3. forty-four dollars and fifty cents _____

4. ninety-nine dollars and ninety-eight cents _____

5. two dollars and eight cents _____

6. one hundred twenty-five dollars _____

7. three hundred twenty-one dollars and seventeen cents _____

8. eight hundred eleven dollars and thirty-four cents _____

C *PAIRS.* Check your answers.

Make It Yours

A Take out your change. Count it. How much change do you have? Write the amount in numbers and words.

> *Example:*
>
> 25¢   *twenty-five cents*
>
> _____ _____

B *PAIRS.* Who has more change, you or your partner?

Listen

48 **Listen. What do you hear? Circle *a*, *b*, or *c*.**

1. **a.**    **b.**    **c.**

2. **a.**   **b.**   **c.**

3. **a.**   **b.**   **c.**

4. **a.** $34.89   **b.** $34.85   **c.** $34.99

5. **a.**    **b.**    **c.**

6. **a.** $115.00   **b.** $150.00   **c.** $155.00

BONUS

Look at the money on page 88.

Who is the man on the one-dollar bill?

Who is the man on the five-dollar bill?

Who is the man on the ten-dollar bill?

Who is the man on the twenty-dollar bill?

Learn

A   *PAIRS.* Look at the receipt. Find these words: *tax, total, change.* What do these words mean?

The Metro Adult School Bookstore	
1 Book	10.50
1 Notebook	2.25
Tax 8%	1.02
Total	13.77
Cash	15.00
Change	1.23

B   Read the receipt. Answer the questions.

1. How much is the book? _____

2. How much is the notebook? _____

3. How much is the tax? _____

4. What's the total? _____

5. How much money did the customer give to the cashier? _____

6. How much change did the customer get? _____

Practice

PAIRS. Answer the questions.

MADISON POST OFFICE
Madison, Wisconsin
53715

Sales Receipt

First-Class Postage $3.89

Total: $3.89

a.

Metro Railroad

Station # 132   Harrison

Harrison to South Falls
         $5.70
Adult, One-way ticket

TOTAL $5.70

Thank you for riding Metro

b.

Metro   HOME   Store

01/22/2006   03:38 PM

783475457
window curtain $38.65

TOTAL $38.65

c.

1. Look at Receipt **a**. You have a five-dollar bill.

   How much change will you get back? _____

2. Look at Receipt **b**. You have a ten-dollar bill.

   How much change will you get back? _____

3. Look at Receipt **c**. You have two twenty-dollar bills.

   How much change will you get back? _____

BONUS   *PAIRS.* Do you have a receipt? Did you pay by cash? Show your receipt to your partner. Did you get the correct change?

Learn

A 🔘 **49** Look. Listen and point. Listen and repeat.

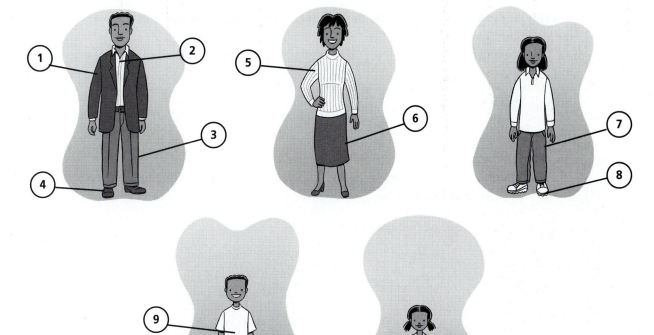

1. jacket	4. shoes	7. jeans	10. shorts
2. shirt	5. sweater	8. sneakers	11. socks
3. pants	6. skirt	9. T-shirt	12. dress

B *PAIRS.* Student A, point to a picture. Student B, say the name of the clothing.

Practice

A Listen to your teacher. Listen and repeat.

A: What's the <u>man</u> wearing?
B: <u>He's</u> wearing <u>a shirt, pants, a jacket, and shoes</u>.

B *PAIRS.* Practice the conversation. Ask and answer questions about the other people in Learn. Take turns.

Make It Yours

A   *PAIRS.*   **What's your partner wearing? Write your answer.**

My partner is _____. _____'s wearing

name

_____.

B   **Tell the class what your partner is wearing. Don't say your partner's name! Class, guess who it is.**

> **Example:**
>
>   A: *My partner is wearing a T-shirt, jeans, and sneakers.*
> Class: *It's Andrea.*

BONUS

What clothes do men wear? What clothes do women wear? What clothes do both men and women wear?

PAIRS.   **Fill in the diagram.**

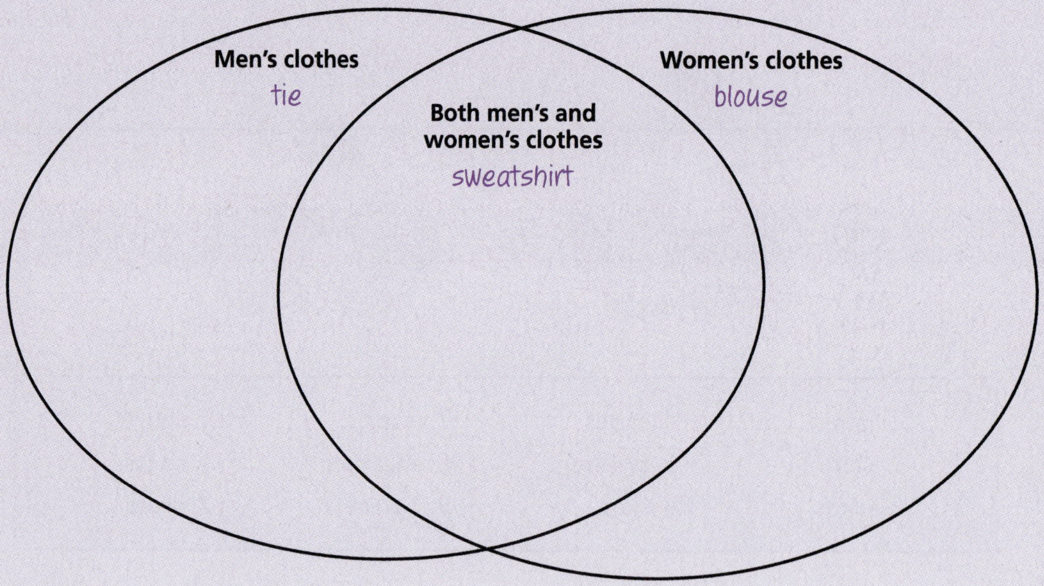

Men's clothes
tie

Both men's and
women's clothes
sweatshirt

Women's clothes
blouse

Learn

A Look at the pictures. Listen to your teacher. Listen and repeat.

small
S

medium
M

large
L

extra large
XL

B *PAIRS.* Student A, point to a T-shirt. Student B, say the size. Take turns.

A: Large.
B: That's right.

Practice

A   50 Listen to the conversation. Listen and repeat.

A: Do you have this T-shirt in a size medium?
B: Just a moment. Yes, we do.
A: Thank you.

B *PAIRS.* Practice the conversation. Use the sizes in Learn and the clothing in the box.

| dress | jacket | shirt | skirt | sweater |

A: Do you have these <u>pants</u> in a size <u>large</u>?
B: Just a moment. No, I'm sorry. We don't.
A: Thanks.

D *PAIRS.* **Practice the conversation. Use the sizes in Learn and the clothing in the box.**

jeans	shorts	socks

Make It Yours

PAIRS. ROLE PLAY. **Student A, you want a sweater in a size small. Ask Student B. Student B, answer *Yes, we do* or *No, I'm sorry. We don't.* You decide!**

Student B, you want a shirt in a size extra large. Ask Student A. Student A, answer *Yes, we do* or *No, I'm sorry. We don't.* You decide!

BONUS **What other clothing can you name? Share your list with the class.**

Lesson 5 Prices

Learn

 52 Look at the ad for Metro Mart. Listen and point. Listen and repeat.

Metro Mart — *One-Day Sale!* —

Women's

Skirts **$25.00**

Hats
Reg. $15.00
Sale **$10.99**

Women's dresses on sale!
Reg. $45.99
Sale **$36.99**

Shoes **$12.99**

Blouses **$30.99**

Men's

Pants
$22.00

Jackets
Reg. $125.99
Sale **$59.99**

Shirts
$19.00

Practice

A   **53** Listen to the conversation. Listen and repeat.

A: How much <u>is</u> the <u>dress</u>?
B: It's <u>$36.99</u>.
A: How much <u>are</u> the <u>pants</u>?
B: They're <u>$22.00</u>.

B *PAIRS.* Practice the conversation. Use the clothes in Learn. Take turns.

BONUS *GROUPS OF 3.* Bring clothing ads to class. Ask and answer questions about the prices of the clothes.

Learn

A 54 ▶ **Look at the picture. Listen and point. Listen and repeat.**

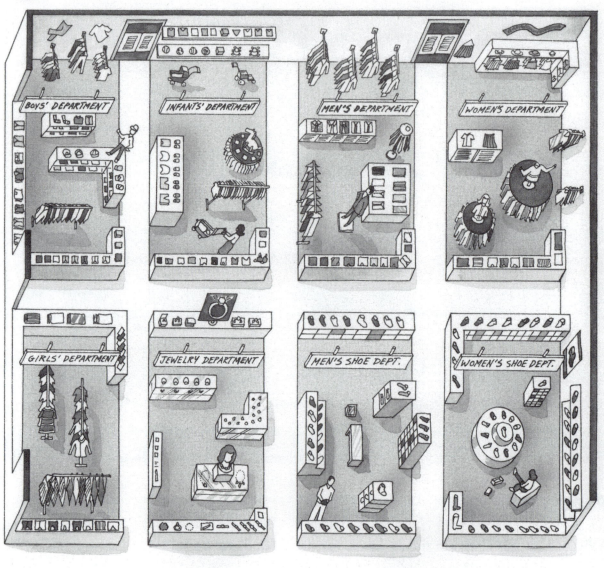

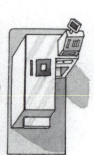

B *PAIRS.* Student A, name a department. Student B, point. Take turns.

Practice

A 55 Listen to the conversation. Listen and repeat.

A: Excuse me. Do you have <u>women's skirts</u>?
B: Yes, we do. They're in the <u>women's department</u>, over there.
A: Thank you.

B *PAIRS.* Practice the conversation. Ask about the items in the box. Use other departments in Learn. Take turns.

baby clothes	girls' jackets	ties
blouses	men's shoes	watches
boys' jeans	rings	women's boots

BONUS Where do you shop for clothes? Ask your classmates. Find a classmate who shops in the same store as you.

Unit 6 Test

Before you take the test

ⒶⒷⒸⒹ Use the answer sheet for Unit 6 on page 215.

1. Print your name.
2. Print your teacher's name.
3. Write your student identification number, and bubble in the information below the boxes.
4. Write the test date and bubble in the information.
5. Write your class number and bubble in the information.

Listening I [Tracks 56–60]

Look at the pictures and listen. What is the correct answer: A, B, or C?

1.

A

B

C

2.

A

B

C

3.

A

B

C

4.

A

B

C

Listening II [Tracks 61–65]

Listen. Everything is on the audio CD.

Reading

Read. What is the correct answer: A, B, C, or D?

TOTAL $3.59

9. What's the total?

   A. three dollars and ninety-five cents

   B. nine dollars and thirty-five cents

   C. three dollars and fifty-nine cents

   D. five dollars and thirty-nine cents

10. How much money is this?

    A. $1.50

    B. $1.60

    C. $1.70

    D. $1.80

The Metro Adult School Bookstore

1 Book	10.50 ①
1 Notebook	2.25
Tax 8%	1.02 ②
Total	13.77
Cash	15.00 ③
Change	1.23 ④

11. Which line shows the tax?

    A. ①

    B. ②

    C. ③

    D. ④

12. How much money did the customer give the cashier?

    A. ①

    B. ②

    C. ③

    D. ④

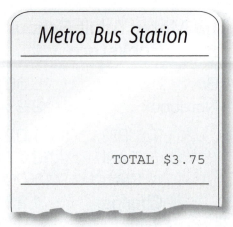

Metro Bus Station

TOTAL $3.75

13. You have a ten-dollar bill. How much change will you get back?

A. $5.25

B. $6.25

C. $8.50

D. $13.75

Unit 7 Food

Learn

A 66 Look at the pictures. Listen and point. Listen and repeat.

oranges   bananas   apples   grapes   pears

cucumbers   carrots   lettuce   tomatoes   onions   potatoes

pie   cake   bread   rolls   cookies

steak   ground beef   pork   turkey   chicken   fish

milk   eggs   cheese   butter

B *PAIRS.* Student A, say a word. Student B, point to the picture.
Take turns.

Practice

A Look at each group of words. Which food does <u>not</u> belong? Write the word.

1. apples, lettuce, oranges, grapes _____

2. tomatoes, ground beef, steak, pork _____

3. milk, cheese, cucumbers, butter _____

4. rolls, pie, cookies, carrots _____

5. turkey, onions, chicken, fish _____

B Look at the words you wrote. Put them together. What do they make?

_____

C Listen to your teacher. Then listen and repeat.

A: Do you like <u>apples</u>?
B: Yes, I do, but I don't like <u>pears</u>.

D Practice the conversation. Use other foods from Learn.

Make It Yours

Find someone who likes each of these foods. Write the person's name.

> *Example:*
>
> *Student A:*   *Antonio, do you like turkey?*
> *Antonio:*   *No, I don't.*
> *Student A:*   *Maria, do you like turkey?*
> *Maria:*   *Yes, I do.*

turkey   <u>Maria _____</u>

potatoes   _____

fish   _____

bananas   _____

BONUS   *PAIRS.* **What do you usually have for lunch? Ask your teacher if you need help with some words.**

Example:

A: What do you usually have for lunch?
B: I usually have a turkey sandwich. What about you?

Learn

A **Look at the pictures. Listen and point. Listen and repeat.**

a can of soup

a jar of tomato sauce

a box of cereal

a bag of potato chips

a bottle of juice

a container of milk

B *PAIRS.* **Student A, say the container. Student B, say the food.**

> *Example:*
> *A: A box of . . .*
> *B: Cereal.*

Practice

GROUPS OF 5. **Play the Supermarket Game.**

A: I'm going to the supermarket. I need a can of tuna.

B: I'm going to the supermarket. I need a can of tuna and a box of cereal.

C: I'm going to the supermarket. I need a can of tuna, a box of cereal, and . . .

Make It Yours

PAIRS. **What other foods do you know? What containers do they go with? Write two foods for each container in Learn.**

Can	Jar	Box	Bag	Bottle	Container

Learn

A Look at the pictures. Listen and point. Listen and repeat.

a dozen

a pound

each

a quart

a half-gallon

a gallon

B Look at the words in the box. Write them in the correct column. Some words can go in more than one column.

| apples | juice | milk | rolls |
| cheese | lettuce | pie | turkey |

A Pound	Each	A Half-Gallon

C *PAIRS.* Check your answers.

Learn

Store-made
Apple Pie

$2.99 ea.

Farmers
Orange Juice

$1.99/qt.

Sunrise
Eggs

99¢/doz.

Kool Iced Tea

99¢/gal.

Mountain
Swiss Cheese

$2.99/lb.

Best Yet
Chocolate Ice Cream

$3.99/½ gal.

Note
> > > > >   *We write $3.99/lb. We say $3.99 a pound* or *$3.99 per pound.*

B   Write the words for each abbreviation.

1. ea.   _____*each*_____
2. qt.   _____
3. doz.   _____
4. gal.   _____
5. lb.   _____
6. ½ gal. _____

C   *PAIRS.* Check your answers.

Practice

A Listen to your teacher. Listen and repeat.

A: How much is the <u>apple pie</u> this week?
B: <u>$2.99</u> each.

B *PAIRS.* Practice the conversation. Use other foods and prices in Learn.

Make It Yours

A Make a list of five foods you usually buy.

Shopping List

eggs

B *PAIRS.* Look at your partner's list. Ask about the prices of the foods. Take turns.

> **Example:**
> A: How much do you usually pay for eggs?
> B: $1.09 a dozen.

BONUS *GROUPS OF 3.* Discuss these questions.

Where do you shop?

Which store has the best prices?

Do you buy all your food in the same store?

Why or why not?

Does everyone in your group agree?

Learn

A **70** **Look at the pictures. Listen and point. Listen and repeat.**

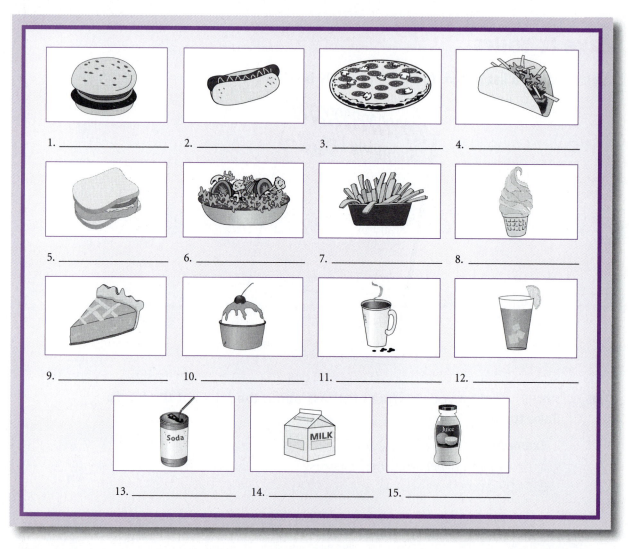

1. _____
2. _____
3. _____
4. _____

5. _____
6. _____
7. _____
8. _____

9. _____
10. _____
11. _____
12. _____

13. _____
14. _____
15. _____

B   **Write the words under the correct picture.**

apple pie	frozen yogurt	ice cream	milk	a sandwich
coffee	a hamburger	iced tea	a pizza	soda
fries	a hot dog	juice	a salad	a taco

C   *PAIRS.* **Check your answers.**

Practice

A **71** **Listen to the conversation. Listen and repeat.**

A: May I take your order?
B: Yes. I'd like <u>a hamburger and fries</u>.
A: Anything else?
B: <u>Coffee</u>, please.

B *PAIRS.* **Practice the conversation. Use different menu items from Learn. Take turns.**

Listen

 72 **Listen. What do you hear? Circle *a*, *b*, or *c*.**

1. a.  b.  c.

2. a.  b.  c.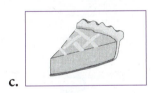

3. a.  b.  c.

4. a.  b.  c.

BONUS Bring in a menu from a restaurant near your school. Role-play a customer and a server at lunchtime.

Unit 7 Test

Listening I [Tracks 73–76]

Look at the pictures and listen. What is the correct answer: A, B, or C?

1.

A

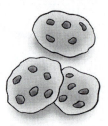
B

C

2.

A

B

C

3.

A

B

C

Listening II [Tracks 77–80]

Listen. Everything is on the audio CD.

Reading

Read. What is the correct answer: A, B, C, or D?

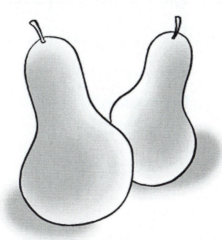

7. What are these?

   A. pears

   B. carrots

   C. tomatoes

   D. potatoes

8. What do you need from the supermarket?

    A. a box of cereal

    B. a can of soup

    C. a jar of tomato sauce

    D. a bag of potatoes

On Sale!

Ground Beef

$3.99/lb.

9. How much is the ground beef?

    A. $3.99 a half-gallon

    B. $3.99 a dozen

    C. $3.99 each

    D. $3.99 a pound

10. May I take your order?

    A. I'd like a hamburger and fries.

    B. I'd like a hamburger, fries, and soda.

    C. I'd like a salad, fries, and juice.

    D. I'd like a hamburger, a salad, and iced tea.

Unit 8 Housing

Learn

A 2 Look at the picture. Listen and point. Listen and repeat.

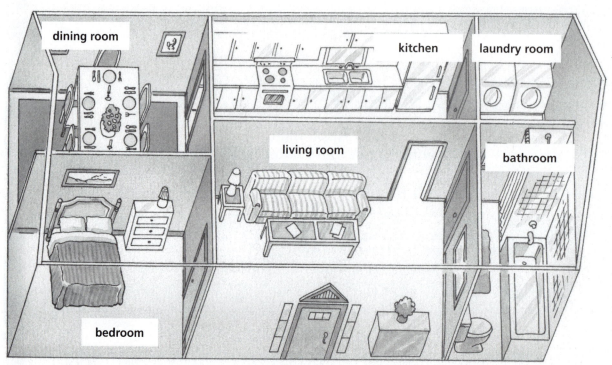

dining room

kitchen

laundry room

living room

bathroom

bedroom

B Match the activities with the rooms.

a.   b.   c.   d.   e.   f.

___b__ 1. laundry room   _____ 3. kitchen   _____ 5. bedroom

_____ 2. living room   _____ 4. dining room   _____ 6. bathroom

C *PAIRS.* Check your answers.

Practice

A **3** **Look at the picture. Listen to the conversation. Listen and repeat.**

A: What's the apartment like?

B: It has <u>one bedroom, a living room, a kitchen, and a bathroom</u>.

A: It sounds nice.

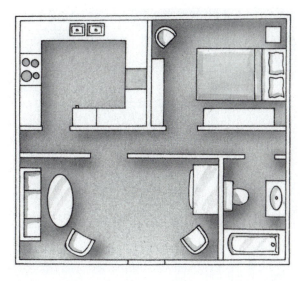

B *PAIRS.* **Practice the conversation. Use the floor plans.**

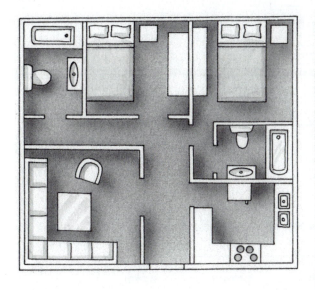

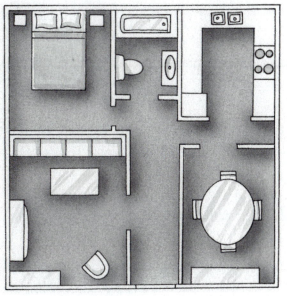

Make It Yours

PAIRS. **Talk about your dream house. Take turns.**

> **Example:**
>
> *A: What's your dream house like?*
> *B: It has three bedrooms and . . .*

Learn

A CD3 TRACK 4 Look at the pictures. Listen and point. Listen and repeat.

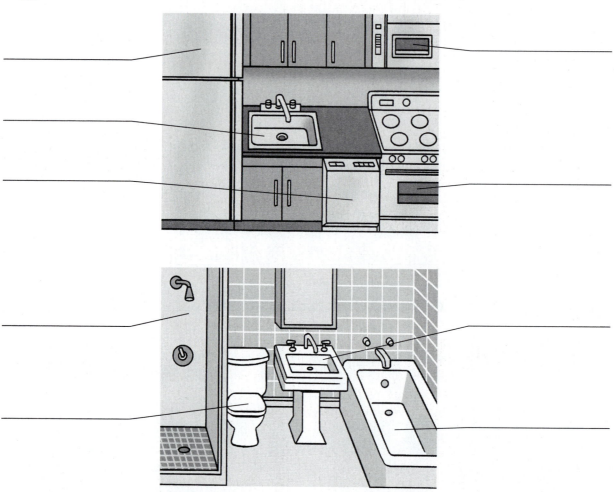

B Write the words on the lines. One word will be used twice.

bathtub	microwave	shower	stove
dishwasher	refrigerator	sink	toilet

C *PAIRS.* Student A, point to a picture. Student B, say the word. Take turns.

Learn

A **5** **Look at the pictures. Listen and point. Listen and repeat.**

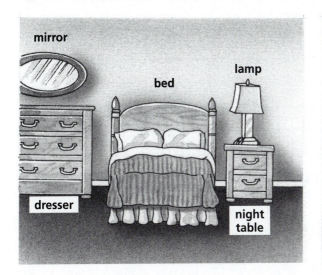

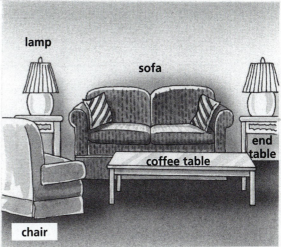

B *PAIRS.* **What furniture is in both the bedroom and the living room?**

_____

Practice

A **Which word does <u>not</u> belong? Cross out the word.**

1. sofa, toilet, lamp, table

2. dishwasher, microwave, bed, stove

3. refrigerator, dresser, table, lamp

4. bathtub, shower, toilet, coffee table

B **Match the words in Exercise A with the rooms in the box.**

bathroom	bedroom	kitchen	~~living room~~

1. _____living room_____

2. _____

3. _____

4. _____

Make It Yours

A What furniture and appliances are in your house? Make a list.

Kitchen	Bathroom	_____ (Room)

B *PAIRS.* Ask about your partner's house. Take turns.

A: What's in your kitchen?

B: There's a refrigerator. . . .

Listen

6 Listen. What do you hear? Circle *a*, *b*, or *c*.

1. **a.** bedroom   **b.** living room   **c.** bathroom

2. **a.** shower   **b.** dresser   **c.** mirror

3. **a.** sink   **b.** stove   **c.** sofa

4. **a.** refrigerator **b.** dishwasher   **c.** sofa

BONUS *GROUPS OF 3.* **What other furniture or appliances do you know? Make a list. Ask your teacher if you need help.**

Kitchen Appliances	Living Room Furniture

Dining Room Furniture	Bedroom Furniture

Learn

A   CD3 TRACK 7   **Look at the pictures. Listen and point. Listen and repeat.**

Marie is washing the dishes.

Robert is cleaning the house.

Soo Yee is doing the laundry.

Rosa is paying the bills.

Peng is cooking dinner.

Seba is shopping for food.

B   *PAIRS.* **Student A, read a sentence. Student B, point to the picture. Take turns.**

Practice

A   **Listen to your teacher. Listen and repeat.**

A: What's <u>Marie</u> doing?
B: <u>She's</u> <u>washing the dishes</u>.

B   *PAIRS.* **Practice the conversation. Use other information from Learn.**

C   *PAIRS.* **Ask about other people. Make new conversations about the people in the box. Use your imagination!**

Marie's husband	Rosa's son
Peng's wife	Soo Yee's daughter

Example:

A: What's Marie's husband doing?
B: He's watching TV.

D   Read Robert's story.

> My wife Cindy and I both work. I'm a salesperson and she's a receptionist. We have two children, Michael and Jennifer. They're in high school.
>
> Everyone helps with the housework and chores. Cindy and I shop for food at the supermarket once a week. Sometimes I cook and sometimes Cindy cooks. Michael and Jennifer wash the dishes. They take turns.
>
> On Saturday, we clean the house. I vacuum, Cindy dusts, and the kids clean their rooms. During the week, I do the laundry and the kids put it away. Cindy pays the bills. She takes care of the money!

E   *PAIRS.* **Read Robert's story again. Answer the questions. Tell your partner.**

1. Who cooks?

2. Who washes the dishes?

3. Who vacuums?

4. Who dusts?

5. Who puts away the laundry?

6. Who pays the bills?

Make It Yours

A   **Work alone. Who does the housework and chores in your house? Write *I* or a family member's name next to each item on the list.**

To do:
cook _____
do the laundry _____
shop for food _____
wash the dishes _____
clean the house _____
pay the bills _____

B   *PAIRS.* **Ask your partner.**

Examples:

A: Who washes the dishes in your house?
B: My mother washes the dishes.

A: Who cooks?
B: I do!

Learn

A   Read the ad. Read the sentences. Circle *T* for *True* or *F* for *False*.

ROOM FOR RENT

Furnished

Utilities included, $300/month

Near transportation

Call 714-555-2234

---

1. There's an apartment for rent.   T (F)
2. It comes with furniture.   T F
3. You have to pay for electricity.   T F
4. The rent is $400 every month.   T F
5. It's near a bus or subway.   T F

B   *PAIRS.* Check your answers.

C   Read the ad. Read the sentences. Circle *T* for *True* or *F* for *False*.

2-Bedroom Apartment for Rent

Large kitchen

No pets

$500/month

Security deposit—1st and last months' rent

Call 714-555-4131

---

1. The apartment has two bedrooms, a living room,
   a kitchen, and a bathroom.   (T) F
2. The kitchen is small.   T F
3. You cannot have a dog.   T F
4. The rent is $500 a month.   T F
5. The security deposit is $1,000.   T F

Practice

A Read the ads. Match the information with the ads. Write the letter of the ad.

a.

1-Bedroom Apartment
Large kitchen
Utilities included
Near a park
$425
Call 777-555-2121

b.

2-Bedroom Apartment
Large dining room
No pets
Security deposit—one month's rent
$750
Call 888-555-3210

2-Bedroom Apartment

1. It has two bedrooms. __b__

2. It has a large kitchen. ____

3. You pay the utilities. ____

4. You can have a pet. ____

5. It's near a park. ____

6. The security deposit is $750. ____

7. The rent is $425. ____

B *PAIRS.* Check your answers.

Learn

A Read the ad. Write the abbreviations for the words.

APT. FOR RENT

2 Br. 2 Ba.
Lg. K., pkg.
Util. incl., furn.
Nr. schools
$1,250/mo.
Call 610-555-1210

1. apartment _____apt._____

2. bathroom _____

3. bedroom _____

4. furnished _____

5. kitchen _____

6. large _____

7. month _____

8. near _____

9. parking _____

10. utilities included _____

B *PAIRS.* Check your answers.

Practice

A Read the ads. Answer the questions. Write the letter of the ad.

a.

Apt. for Rent

2 BR, Lg. K., Nr. trans.

$775/mo.

Call 516-555-3456

b.

Apt. for Rent

1 BR, furn., util. incl.

$400/mo.

Call 615-555-4321

1. Which ad is for a two-bedroom apartment? _a_

2. Which ad is for a furnished apartment? _____

3. Which apartment has a large kitchen? _____

4. Which apartment is near transportation? _____

5. Which apartment includes utilities? _____

B *PAIRS.* Check your answers.

Make It Yours

A Write an ad for your home. (It's OK to use made-up information.)

_____ **FOR RENT**

_____ incl.

_____ BR _____ BA

nr. _____

_____ /mo.

B *PAIRS.* Show your ad to your partner. Describe your home. Take turns.

Example:

A: My apartment has two bedrooms. It is . . .

BONUS **GROUPS OF 3.** Bring the classified ad section from your newspaper to school. Share it with the group. Find a place to live near the school, and talk about it with your group.

Unit 8 Test

Listening I [Tracks 8–11]

Look at the pictures and listen. What is the correct answer: A, B, or C?

1.

    A   B   C

2.

    A   B   C

3.

    A   B   C

Listening II [Tracks 12–15]

Listen. Everything is on the audio CD.

Reading

Read. What is the correct answer: A, B, C, or D?

---

7. It's in the living room.

    A. ①

    B. ②

    C. ③

    D. ④

8. Vanessa wants a new mirror.

    A. ①

    B. ②

    C. ③

    D. ④

9. What is he doing?

    A. He's washing the dishes.

    B. He's cleaning the house.

    C. He's doing the laundry.

    D. He's cooking dinner.

Apt. for Rent

2 BR, util incl, pets OK

$550/mo.

security deposit 1st and last mo.

nr. trans, available now

Call 608-555-1212

---

10. How many bedrooms are there?

    A. one

    B. two

    C. three

    D. four

11. How much is the security deposit?

    A. $550

    B. $1,100

    C. $225

    D. $1,212

Unit 9 Talking on the Phone

135

Lesson 1 — Making Personal Calls

Learn

 16 Look at the picture. Listen to the conversation. Point to the person speaking.

Practice

 A **17** Listen to the conversation again. Listen and repeat.

A: Hello?
B: Hi. This is <u>Elena</u>. May I speak to Lan?
A: Yes. Hold on, please.

B *PAIRS.* Practice the conversation. Student B, use your own name. Ask for Lan.

Learn

 18 Look at the picture. Listen to the conversation. Point to the person speaking.

Practice

 A **19** Listen to the conversation again. Listen and repeat.

A: Hello?
B: Hi. This is Ricardo. Is Marta there?
A: No, I'm sorry. She isn't here.
     Can I take a message?
B: Yes. Please ask her to call Ricardo.

B Look at the messages. Put a check (✓) under the message that matches the second conversation on page 136.

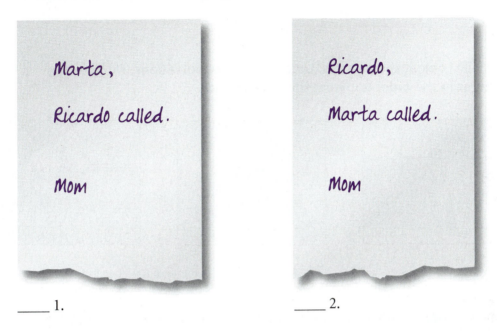

Marta,

Ricardo called.

Mom

_____ 1.

Ricardo,

Marta called.

Mom

_____ 2.

Make It Yours

PAIRS. Practice the conversation. Student B, use your own name. Student A, take a message. Write your own name.

_____,

_____.

_____.

_____

BONUS How do you answer the phone in your country? Share your answer with the class.

Learn

A 🔘 **20** Look at the pictures. Listen to the conversations. Number the pictures in the order you hear them described.

_____   _____   _____

B 🔘 **21** Look at the messages. Listen to the conversations again. Write the phone numbers.

While You Were Out

To: _Dr. Sanders_   From: _Ming Tan_

Time: _1:00 P.M._   Date: _Jan. 4_

Message: _Please call_   Phone: _____

a.

While You Were Out

To: _Ms. Grover_

From: _Marta Gomez_

Time: _3:30 P.M._

Date: _5/15_

Message: _Please call_

Phone: _____

b.

While You Were Out

To: _Mr. Pacer_   From: _Bob Carey_

Time: _10:00 A.M._   Date: _6/10_

Message: _Please call_

Phone: _____

c.

C 🔘 **22** **Listen to the conversation. Listen and repeat.**

A: Metro Business Machines. This is <u>Edgar</u>.
B: Hello. Is Mr. Pacer there?
A: I'm sorry. He's not in. May I take your name and number?
B: Yes. My name is <u>Bob Carey</u> and my number is <u>212-555-8541</u>.
A: I'll give him the message. Thank you for calling. Good-bye.

D *PAIRS.* Practice the conversation. Use your names and number.
Take turns.

Practice

A *PAIRS.* Make a conversation. Use the information in the message.
Fill in the lines below.

Wee Care Day Care ☀

While You Were Out

To: _____Emma Wong_____   From: _Ricardo Gomez_

Date: _____5/05_____   Time: _____2:30 P.M._____

Message: _Please call_   Phone: _213-555-4455_

A: _____. This is Linda.

B: Hello. Is _____ there?

A: I'm sorry. _____ not in. May I take _____?

B: Yes. My name is _____ and my number is _____.

A: I'll give _____ the message. Thank you for calling. Good-bye.

B *PAIRS.* Practice the conversation. Use your names and numbers.
Take turns.

BONUS *GROUPS OF 3.* What businesses do you call? How do the people at the business answer the phone?

Learn

A **23** Look at the pictures. Listen and point. Listen and repeat.

_____ I have a flat tire.   _____ My mother is in the hospital.   _____ My son is sick.

_____ I'm sick.   _____ There's a lot of traffic.   _____ I had an accident.

B **24** Look at the pictures again. Listen to the conversations.
Write *A* (absent) on the line if the person isn't going to go to work.
Write *L* (late) if the person is going to be late.

C *WITH THE CLASS.* Who has a good reason for being absent or late?
Point to the pictures. Explain.

D **25** Listen to the conversations. Listen and repeat.

A: Metro Phone Company.
B: Hi. This is <u>Peter</u>. <u>I can't come to work today</u>. <u>I'm sick</u>.
  Please tell Mr. Lee.
A: OK. I'll give him the message.

A: Metro Department Store.
B: Hi. This is <u>Anita</u>. <u>I'm going to be late</u>. <u>I have a flat tire</u>.
  Please tell Ms. Posen.
A: OK. I'll give her the message.

Practice

PAIRS. Practice the conversations in Learn. Give different reasons for being late or absent. Use the reasons in Learn. Take turns.

Make It Yours

A   *PAIRS.* Why are you absent or late for work? Why are you absent or late for school? Fill in the chart.

Name	Work: Absent	Work: Late	School: Absent	School: Late

B   *PAIRS.* Write a conversation. Tell why you are late or absent for work or school. Use reasons from Exercise A.

C   *PAIRS.* Role-play your conversation for the class.

Listen

 26 Listen to reasons why three people are going to be late or absent. Read the statements. Listen again and then circle *T* for *True* or *F* for *False*.

1. Jack has a flat tire.   T   F

2. Patty's husband is in the hospital.   T   F

3. Amanda is sick.   T   F

BONUS   *WITH THE CLASS.* Are there different reasons for being late or absent in different countries?

Unit 9 Test

Before you take the test

Ⓐ Ⓑ Ⓒ Ⓓ Use the answer sheet for Unit 9 on page 221.

1. Print your name.
2. Print your teacher's name.
3. Write your student identification number, and bubble in the information below the boxes.
4. Write the test date and bubble in the information.
5. Write your class number and bubble in the information.

Listening I [Tracks 27–30]

Look at the pictures and listen. What is the correct answer: A, B, or C?

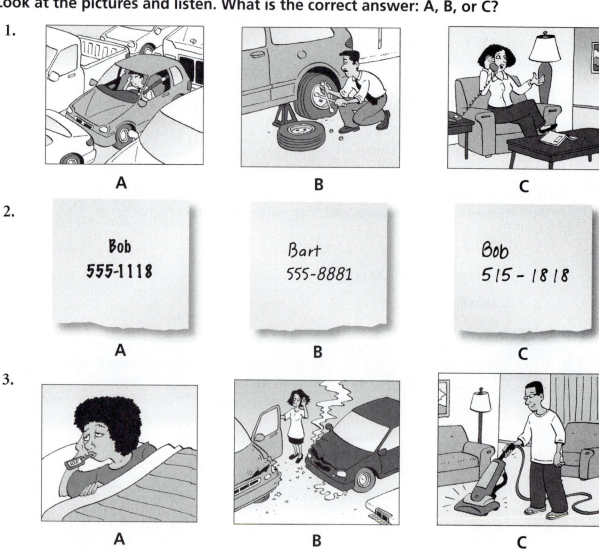

1.

A   B   C

2.

Bob
555-1118

Bart
555-8881

Bob
515-1818

A   B   C

3.

A   B   C

Listening II [Tracks 31–34]

Listen. Everything is on the audio CD.

Reading

Read. What is the correct answer: A, B, C, or D?

7. What does the woman answer?

   A. No, she isn't. Can I take a message?

   B. No, I can't.

   C. May I speak to Lucy?

   D. Please ask her to call Jim.

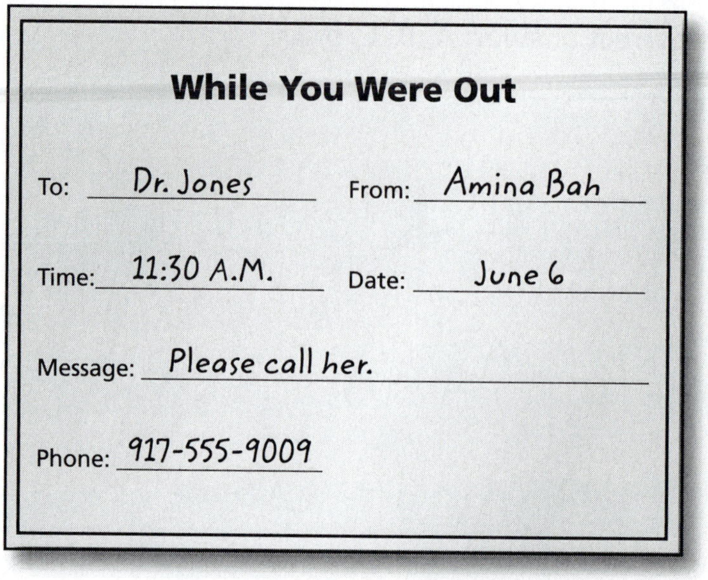

While You Were Out

To: _Dr. Jones_ From: _Amina Bah_

Time: _11:30 A.M._ Date: _June 6_

Message: _Please call her._

Phone: _917-555-9009_

---

8. Who called?

A. Dr. Jones

B. Amina Bah

C. 11:30 A.M.

D. June 6

9. What is the message?

A. Call Dr. Jones.

B. Dr. Jones needs to call Amina.

C. Amina will call again.

D. Amina's appointment is at 11:30.

10. Why is the man going to be late?

    A. He's in the hospital.

    B. He has a flat tire.

    C. There's a lot of traffic.

    D. He's sick.

11. Why can't the man come to work today?

    A. He's doing the laundry.

    B. He has a flat tire.

    C. He had an accident.

    D. His son is sick.

Unit 10 Health

Learn

A   **35** Look at the picture. Listen and point. Listen and repeat.

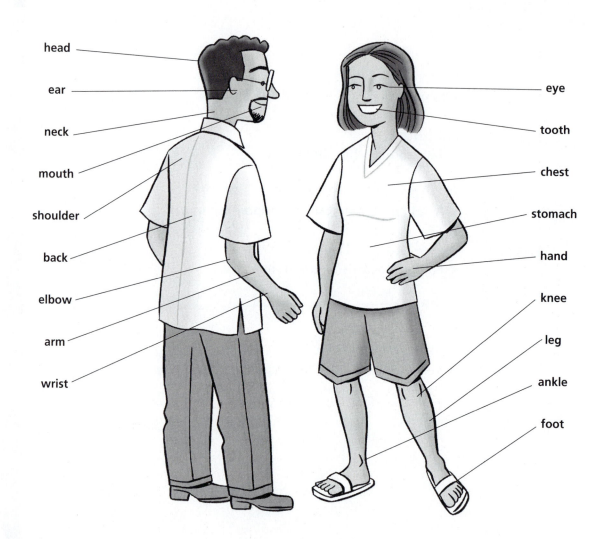

head

ear

neck

mouth

shoulder

back

elbow

arm

wrist

eye

tooth

chest

stomach

hand

knee

leg

ankle

foot

B   Circle any words that are new to you.

C   *PAIRS.* Read the new words to your partner. Are any of your words the same?

Practice

PAIRS. Student A, say a part of the body. Student B, point to it. Take turns.

Example:

A: *Touch your head.*

B:

Make It Yours

A   Look at the picture. Label the parts of the body.

B   *PAIRS.* Check your answers.

BONUS   Do you know the words for any other parts of the body? Write the words on the picture.

Lesson 2 Feeling Sick

Learn

A Match the pictures with the sentences.

 a.

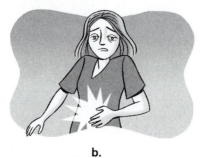 b.

 c.

d.

e.

_____ 1. I have a headache.

_____ 2. I have an earache.

_____ 3. I have a toothache.

_____ 4. I have a backache.

_____ 5. I have a stomachache.

B CD3 TRACK 36 Listen and check your answers. Listen and repeat.

C _PAIRS._ Student A, show an ache. Student B, say which ache it is. Take turns.

Example:

A:

B: A stomachache!
A: You're right!

37 **Look at the pictures. Listen and point. Listen and repeat.**

a cold   a cough   a fever   the flu   a sore throat

E   **Look at the pictures. Complete the sentences.**

1. I have _____.

2. I have _____.

3. I have _____.

4. I have _____.

5. I have _____.

F   **38** **Listen and check your answers. Listen and repeat.**

Practice

A Which five words go with *-ache*? Write the new words on the lines.

arm	~~ear~~	head	shoulder	tooth
back	foot	knee	stomach	wrist

1. ___earache___ 2. _____ 3. _____ 4. _____ 5. _____

B Which words go with *a*? Which word goes with *the*? Write *a* or *the* on the lines.

1. _____ cold

2. _____ fever

3. _____ sore throat

4. _____ cough

5. _____ flu

Make It Yours

A CD3 TRACK 39 Listen to the conversation. Listen and repeat.

A: What's the matter?
B: I have <u>a headache</u> and <u>a sore throat</u>.
A: I'm sorry.

B *PAIRS.* Practice the conversation with other problems in Practice. Show the problem. Take turns.

C CD3 TRACK 40 Listen to the conversation. Listen and repeat.

A: What's the matter?
B: My <u>shoulder</u> hurts.
A: I'm sorry.

D *PAIRS.* Practice the conversation with other parts of the body. (Hint: Look again at page 150.) Take turns.

Listen

 41 Listen. What do you hear? Circle *a*, *b*, or *c*.

1.   **a.**   **b.**   **c.**

2.   **a.**   **b.**   **c.**

3.   **a.**   **b.**   **c.**

BONUS   *TEAMS OF 3.* **Look at these sentence starters. Write as many sentences as you can for each one. Use words from Lessons 1 and 2. You have 5 minutes.**

Example:

I have a headache. My shoulder hurts.

I have a _____.

I have the _____.

My _____ hurts.

Which team had the most correct sentences?

Learn

A   Match the appointment cards with the sentences.

Jim Schwartz
has an appointment with
Janet Reid, M.D.
TEL: 202-555-1982

DATE: _____ 9/30 _____

TIME: _____ 3:45 P.M. _____

MON. ___ TUES. ___ WED. ___ THURS. ___ FRI. X

a.

Amy Wittier
has an appointment on

Mon.	Feb.	2
day	month	date

at _____ 11:30 _____ A.M. P.M.

b.

Joan

My appointment is on

M   T   W   TH   F

DATE: 7/16 AT: 4:00 A.M. (P.M.)

c.

Robert Delgado
You have an appointment with

Dr. Nicholas Silver

Tues.	April	18
day	month	date

at _____ 10:15 _____ A.M. P.M.

d.

_____ 1. Your next appointment is on Friday, September 30, at 3:45 in the afternoon.

_____ 2. Your next appointment is on Thursday, July 16, at 4:00 P.M.

_____ 3. Your next appointment is on Tuesday, April 18, at 10:15 in the morning.

_____ 4. Your next appointment is on Monday, February 2, at 11:30 A.M.

Note
>>>>>   *If you can't go to an appointment, always call the day before to tell the doctor's office. If you don't call, sometimes you have to pay!*

B CD3 TRACK 42 **Look at the appointment cards. Listen. Number the cards in the order of the appointments you hear.**

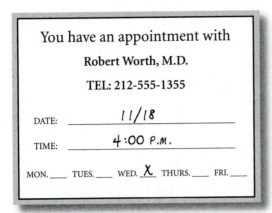

You have an appointment with

Robert Worth, M.D.

TEL: 212-555-1355

DATE: _____ 11/18 _____

TIME: _____ 4:00 P.M. _____

MON. ____ TUES. ____ WED. _X_ THURS. ____ FRI. ____

_____

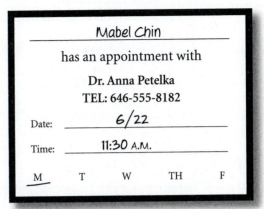

_____ **Mabel Chin** _____

has an appointment with

Dr. Anna Petelka
TEL: 646-555-8182

Date: _____ 6/22 _____

Time: _____ 11:30 A.M. _____

_M_   T   W   TH   F

_____

_____ **Eva Grant** _____

has an appointment on

Friday   _Mar._   _10_
day   month   date

at _____ 9 A.M. _____

_____

Remember

See Unit 4 for abbreviations for days and months.

Practice

A CD3 TRACK 43 **Listen to the conversation. Listen and repeat.**

A: Your next appointment is on <u>Friday, March 10</u>, at <u>9 o'clock</u>.
B: OK. That's Friday, March 10, at 9 o'clock.
A: That's right.

B *PAIRS.* **Practice the conversation with other days, dates, and times. Take turns.**

Make It Yours

A **44** Look at the appointment cards. Listen and complete them.

1.
You have an appointment
with

Dr. David Pound
TEL: 618-555-1326

Date: _____

Time: _____

M _____ T _____ W _____ Th _____ F _____

2.
Dr. Reuben Iwanaga
Honolulu Health Clinic
Honolulu, HI 96801

_____

DAY   MONTH   DATE

AT _____ A.M./P.M.

B *PAIRS.* Student A, tell Student B a date and time. Student B, complete the appointment card. Write your name on the top line. Take turns.

Example:

A: Your next appointment is on Tuesday, May 11, at 3:15.
B: Tuesday, May 11, at 3:15?
A: That's right.

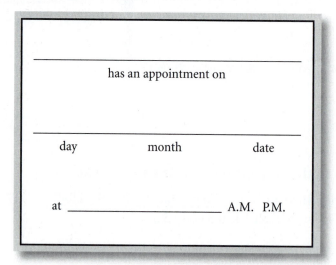

_____

has an appointment on

_____

day   month   date

at _____ A.M. P.M.

Listen

 45 Listen. What do you hear? Circle *a*, *b*, or *c*.

1. **a.** Thursday   **b.** Saturday   **c.** Tuesday

2. **a.** May 3   **b.** May 30   **c.** May 13

3. **a.** 2:00   **b.** 12:00   **c.** 10:00

Learn

 46 Look at the pictures. Listen and point. Listen and repeat.

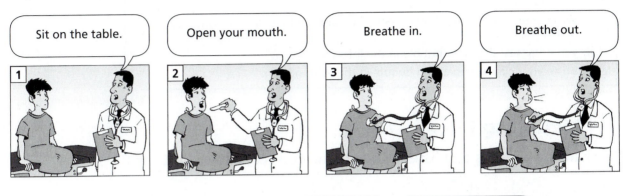

Sit on the table.	Open your mouth.	Breathe in.	Breathe out.
1	2	3	4

Step on the scale.	Lie down.	Look straight ahead.
5	6	7

Practice

A PAIRS. Student A, say a sentence from Learn. Student B, do the action. Take turns.

Example:

A: Open your mouth.

B:

B Cover the exercise in Learn. Complete the sentences.

1. _____ on the scale.

2. _____ your mouth.

3. _____ on the table.

Unit 10 Test

Before you take the test

Ⓐ Ⓑ Ⓒ Ⓓ Use the answer sheet for Unit 10 on page 223.

1. Print your name.
2. Print your teacher's name.
3. Write your student identification number, and bubble in the information below the boxes.
4. Write the test date and bubble in the information.
5. Write your class number and bubble in the information.

Listening I [Tracks 47–50]

Look at the pictures and listen. What is the correct answer: A, B, or C?

1.

| A | B | C |

2.

| A | B | C |

3.

Tues.	April	19
DAY	MONTH	DATE
3:00 P.M.		
TIME		

Thurs.	March	3
DAY	MONTH	DATE
5:00 P.M.		
TIME		

Tues.	April	3
DAY	MONTH	DATE
10:00 A.M.		
TIME		

| A | B | C |

Listening II [Tracks 51–54]

Listen. Everything is on the audio CD.

Reading

Read. What is the correct answer: A, B, C, or D?

7. Touch your foot.

    A. ①

    B. ②

    C. ③

    D. ④

8. What's the matter?

    A. He has a backache.

    B. He has a stomachache.

    C. He has a headache.

    D. He has a sore throat.

Sandra Case

You have an appointment with

Sarah Lee, M.D.

TEL: 718-555-3000

DATE: _____ 4/19 _____

TIME: _____ 8:30 A.M. _____

MON. ___ TUES. ___ WED. ___ THURS. ___ FRI. X SAT. ___

9. When is Sandra's appointment?

A. Friday evening

B. Saturday afternoon

C. Saturday morning

D. Friday morning

10. What time is the appointment?

A. at 8:30

B. on April 19

C. with Dr. Lee

D. on Friday

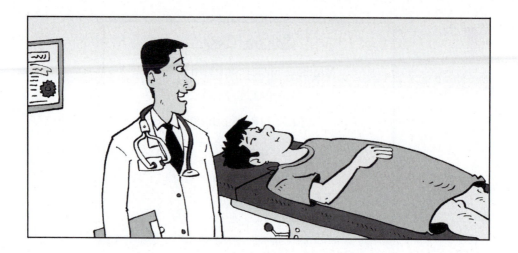

11. What was the doctor's instruction?

    A. Sit on the table.

    B. Lie down.

    C. Step on the scale.

    D. His arm hurts.

Unit 11 Safety Procedures

Learn

A

  55 Look at the pictures. Listen and point. Listen and repeat.

a.　　　b.　　　c.　　　d.　　　e.　　　f.

B *PAIRS.* Student A, read a sign out loud. Student B, point to the picture. Take turns.

Practice

A Match the sign in Learn with the definition. Write the letter.

_____ 1. You can't smoke here.　　　_____ 4. You can't park here.

_____ 2. Be careful. The floor is slippery.　　_____ 5. Use this door to leave.

_____ 3. This place is not safe.　　　_____ 6. You can't go in there.

B *PAIRS.* Check your answers.

> **Example:**
> *A: What does* Danger *mean?*
> *B: It means* This place is not safe.

Make It Yours

Where do you see the signs in Learn? Write the names of the signs in the correct column.

Outside	Inside	Both

BONUS *PAIRS.* What other safety signs do you see in your school? Walk around your school. Copy the signs. Share them with the class.

Lesson 2 — Safety Warnings

Learn

A **56** Look at the pictures. Listen and point. Listen and repeat.

Wait!

Stop!

Watch out!

Be careful!

Walk. Don't run!

Don't touch!

B *PAIRS.* Student A, point to a picture. Student B, say the warning. Take turns.

Practice

A Look at the pictures. Write a different warning from Learn for each picture. More than one answer is possible.

1. _____ 2. _____ 3. _____ 4. _____

B *PAIRS.* Are your answers the same?

Listen

 Listen. What do you hear? Circle *a* or *b*.

1.   **a.** Wait!   **b.** Walk!

2.   **a.** Stop!   **b.** Wait!

3.   **a.** Be careful!   **b.** Watch out!

4.   **a.** Don't run!   **b.** Don't touch!

BONUS   *GROUPS OF 3.* **What other warnings in English do you know? Share them with the class.**

Learn

58 Look at the pictures. Listen and point. Listen and repeat.

1. Close the windows and doors.

2. Leave everything in the room.

3. Walk calmly to the exit.

4. Take the stairs. Do not take the elevator.

5. Stay away from the building.

6. Wait for the fire department.

Practice

A Read the sentences. Circle *T* for *True* or *F* for *False*.

If you hear the fire alarm, you should . . .

1. stay in the room.   T (F)
2. take the elevator.   T   F
3. open the windows.   T   F
4. close the door.   T   F
5. walk to the exit.   T   F

B *PAIRS.* Check your answers.

Make It Yours

Imagine that there's a fire! Have a fire drill.

Learn

Read the instructions for earthquake safety.

1. 2. 3. 4.

1. Stay away from mirrors, windows, tall bookcases, and shelves.
2. Duck! Duck under a desk, table, or doorway.
3. Cover! Stay under cover until the shaking stops.
4. Hold! Hold on to the desk or table.

Practice

A Look at the pictures. Check (✓) *Do* or *Don't*.

1. 2. 3.

1. Do ☐   Don't ☐   2. Do ☐   Don't ☐   3. Do ☐   Don't ☐

B *PAIRS.* Check your answers.

Make It Yours

Imagine that there's an earthquake! Duck! Cover! Hold!

Lesson 5 · Call 911

Learn

 59 Look at the pictures. Listen and point. Listen and repeat.

1. My friend is having a heart attack.

2. There was an accident.

3. There was a robbery.

4. There's a fire.

Practice

A **60** Listen to the conversation. Listen and repeat.

A: This is 911. What's your emergency?
B: <u>My friend is having a heart attack.</u>
A: Where are you?
B: 222 Park Street, Apartment 6C.

B *PAIRS.* Practice the conversation. Use other emergencies from Learn.

Note >>>>> *Call 911 only for emergencies. Call the police department for other problems.*

BONUS *GROUPS OF 3.* **What other 911 emergencies do you know?**

Unit 11 Test

Listening I [Tracks 61–64]

Look at the pictures and listen. What is the correct answer: A, B, or C?

1.

A

B

C

2.

A

B

C

3.

A

B

C

Listening II [Tracks 65–68]

Listen. Everything is on the audio CD.

Reading

Read. What is the correct answer: A, B, C, or D?

7. What does this sign mean?

    A. Exit here.

    B. Be careful.

    C. You can't smoke here.

    D. You can't park here.

8. What is the warning?

    A. Don't go in there.

    B. Walk. Don't run!

    C. The floor is slippery.

    D. Don't touch!

In Case of Fire

9. Leave everything in the room.

    A. ①

    B. ②

    C. ③

    D. ④

10. Stay away from the building.

    A. ①

    B. ②

    C. ③

    D. ④

11. What does this picture mean?

    A. Stay away from windows.

    B. Duck under a table.

    C. Stay under cover.

    D. Hold on to the desk.

Unit 12 Employment

Learn

A **69** Look at the pictures. Listen and point. Listen and repeat.

1. bus driver	4. doctor	7. musician	10. plumber
2. construction worker	5. housekeeper	8. office clerk	11. salesperson
3. cook	6. lawyer	9. painter	12. waiter

B **PAIRS.** Student A, point to a picture. Student B, say the occupation. Take turns.

Practice

A Look at the pictures. Read the statements. Circle *T* for *True* or *F* for *False*.

 1.

 2.

 3.

 4.

5.

 6.

1. He's a ~~musician~~.   T   **(F)**   _bus driver_

2. She's a construction worker.   T   F   _____

3. She's a salesperson.   T   F   _____

4. She's a housekeeper.   T   F   _____

5. He's a doctor.   T   F   _____

6. He's a plumber.   T   F   _____

B **PAIRS. Check your answers. Write the correct answers.**

C 🔊 **70 Listen to the conversation. Listen and repeat.**

A: What do you do?
B: I'm a <u>cook</u>. What do you do?
A: I'm a <u>plumber</u>.

D **PAIRS. Role play. Practice the conversation. Use other occupations in Learn.**

Make It Yours

A **PAIRS. Student A, ask your partner *What do you do?* Student B, give a true answer. Take turns.**

B **Report to the class.**

> **Example:**
>
> *Lily is a housekeeper.*

Learn

A **71** **Listen and read the sentences. Listen and repeat.**

1. Mr. Diaz gives legal help and goes to court.

2. Mai Lin cleans hotel rooms and makes beds.

3. Bob serves food and drinks.

4. Ms. Teller prepares food.

5. Mrs. Rodriguez sells clothes.

6. John fixes sinks and toilets.

7. Susan builds houses.

8. Dr. Roberts takes care of sick people.

9. Monica answers the phone and uses the computer.

10. Mr. Benson drives a bus.

11. Fred paints houses.

12. Ms. Li plays the violin.

B *PAIRS.* **Student A, say a sentence about a picture. Student B, say the occupation.**

> **Example:**
>
> *A: Ms. Teller prepares food.*
> *B: She's a cook.*

Practice

A 72 Listen to the conversation. Listen and repeat.

A: What does <u>Bob</u> do?
B: He's a <u>waiter</u>. He <u>serves food and drinks</u>.

B *PAIRS.* Practice the conversation. Use the occupations in Learn.

Make It Yours

A *PAIRS.* Student A, ask your partner *What job do you want?*
Student B, give a true answer. Take turns.

> *Example:*
> *I want to be a bus driver.*

B Report to the class.

> *Example:*
> *Rosario wants to be a bus driver.*

Listen

73 Listen. What do you hear? Circle *a*, *b*, or *c*.

1. **a.** bus driver   **b.** cook   **c.** waiter
2. **a.** doctor   **b.** construction worker   **c.** housekeeper
3. **a.** lawyer   **b.** doctor   **c.** waiter
4. **a.** plumber   **b.** construction worker   **c.** office clerk
5. **a.** salesperson   **b.** lawyer   **c.** bus driver

BONUS Bring in pictures of people doing different jobs. Write two sentences for each picture.

> *Example:*
> She's a dentist.
> She takes care of people's teeth.
>
> _____
>
> _____
>
> _____

Learn

A Read the ads. Read the sentences. Look at the words in bold. Correct the mistakes.

Grandpa's Restaurant

Waiters full time

Must have experience

M-F 6:00 A.M.–2:00 P.M.

Apply in person

Gabe's Plumbing

Part-time plumbers needed

Immediate openings

License required

Call 562-666-4321

1. Grandpa's Restaurant needs ~~cooks~~. _____waiters_____
2. Gabe's Plumbing needs **teachers**. _____
3. The waiter job is **four** days a week. _____
4. You need **a car** for the plumber job. _____
5. For the waiter job, you should **call**. _____
6. For the plumber job, you should **apply online**. _____

B *PAIRS.* Check your answers.

Learn

A Match the words with the abbreviations.

1. _c_ P/T   a. license
2. ____ F/T   b. required
3. ____ exp.   c. part-time
4. ____ req.   d. experience
5. ____ lic.   e. full-time

B *PAIRS.* Check your answers.

C Read the ads. Read the sentences. Match the jobs with the sentences.
Write *a* or *b*.

Metro Hotel
P/T housekeeper
Exp. req.
Apply online at
metrohotel@city.com
or call 234-555-9876

a.

Dante's Pizza

F/T delivery person

12:00–8:00

Driver's lic. req.

Apply in person

b.

1. The job is part-time.   *a*

2. The job is full-time.   _____

3. You need a driver's license.   _____

4. You need experience.   _____

5. You have to apply in person. _____

D *PAIRS.* Check your answers.

Make It Yours

A Write an ad for a job you want. Use abbreviations if possible.

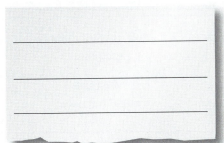

B *PAIRS.* Look at your partner's ad. Ask questions about the job.

> *Examples:*
> *What are the hours? Where is it? Is it part-time or full-time?*

BONUS Is there a bulletin board in your school? Are there any ads on it?
Ask your teacher if your school has a career center.

Note
>>>>> *In a job interview, it is important to speak clearly, to look at the person interviewing you, and to give a firm handshake. If you do not have a skill or experience, you can say, No, I can't, but I can learn.*

Example:
A: Can you <u>drive a bus</u>?
B: No, I can't, but I can learn.

Learn

 74 Look at the picture. Listen to the interview. Point to the person speaking.

Practice

A **75** Listen to the interview again. Listen and repeat.

A: Tell me about your work experience.
B: I can <u>drive a truck</u>.
   I've been a <u>truck driver</u> for five years.

B *PAIRS.* Practice the conversation.

C *PAIRS.* Practice the conversation again. Use the words in the box.

lift heavy boxes stockroom clerk	take care of children nanny	take care of plants gardener
use a cash register cashier	use a computer office assistant	fix cars auto mechanic

Make It Yours

PAIRS. Role-play a job interview. (It's OK to use made-up information.)

BONUS **GROUPS OF 3.** Talk about jobs that you had in your country. (It's OK to use made-up information.) Write down the experience you have. Share it with the class.

Lesson 5 Work Schedules

Learn

A **76** Read the work schedule. Listen and point to the information.

Metro Department Store Work Schedule
Week: April 10–April 17

Name	Department	Days	Hours
Brady, Tom	shoes	Wed.–Sat.	9:00–1:00
Gomez, Maria	dresses	Sun., Mon., Tues., Thurs.	12:00–8:30
Nam, Lin	ladies' coats	Mon.–Fri.	1:00–5:00
Perez, Ricardo	office	Sat. & Sun.	8:00–4:00

B **77** Listen again. Answer the questions.

1. How do we say "–" ? (for example, Wed. – Sat.) _____
2. How do we say "&" ? (for example, Sat. & Sun.) _____

Practice

A *PAIRS.* Look at the schedule in Learn. Ask and answer questions about the people. Take turns.

A: Who works <u>Wednesday to Saturday</u>?
B: <u>Tom Brady.</u>
A: What are his hours?
B: <u>Nine to one.</u>

B Look at the schedule in Learn. What are the people's days off?
(A day off = no work.) Complete the chart.

Name	Days Off
Brady, Tom	Sunday, Monday, Tuesday
Gomez, Maria	
Nam, Lin	
Perez, Ricardo	

C *PAIRS.* Check your answers.

Listen

 Listen. Complete the work schedule.

World Diner
Work Week of April 24–May 1

Name	Days Working	Hours Working
Albers, Mark	Mon., _____, Fri., _____	_____ –3:00
Bart, Sue	_____ –Sat.	9:00– _____
Lopez, Sonya	_____	_____ –10:00
Tran, Lin	Wed.– _____	_____ –5:00

Learn

Look at Ricardo's schedule. Answer the questions.

Perez, Ricardo

Time

8:00–10:00	Office
10:00–10:15	Break
10:15–12:00	Office
12:00–12:45	Lunch
12:45–2:15	Office
2:15–2:30	Break
2:30–4:00	Office

1. What time is Ricardo's lunch? _____

2. How long does he get for lunch? _____

3. When are his breaks? _____

4. How long is each break? _____

5. How many hours a day does Ricardo work? _____

Make It Yours

A Show your schedule for a week. Check (✓) the hours you go to school or go to work each day of the week.

		A.M.			P.M.						A.M.		
		6–8	8–10	10–12	12–2	2–4	4–6	6–8	8–10	10–12	12–2	2–4	4–6
Mon.	Work:												
	School:												
Tues.	Work:												
	School:												
Wed.	Work:												
	School:												
Thurs.	Work:												
	School:												
Fri.	Work:												
	School:												
Sat.	Work:												
	School:												
Sun.	Work:												
	School:												

B *PAIRS.* Share your weekly schedule.

C Write your school or work schedule for a day. When is your lunch hour? When are your breaks? (See Ricardo's schedule on page 184.)

> *Example:*
> 9:00–10:15   School
> 10:15–10:30   Break

D *PAIRS.* Share your daily schedule.

BONUS *WITH THE CLASS.* Discuss different jobs and different types of schedules. What hours do doctors work? Nurses? What jobs have 24-hour schedules?

Lesson 6 — Reporting Problems on the Job

Learn

A   **Look at the pictures. Complete the sentences. Use the words in the box.**

cash register	detergent	sugar
computer	oven	~~paper~~

1. We're out of
   _____ paper _____ .

2. We're out of
   _____ .

3. We're out of
   _____ .

4. The _____
   isn't working.

5. The _____
   isn't working.

6. The _____
   isn't working.

B   **Listen and check your answers. Listen again and repeat.**

C   *PAIRS.* **Answer the questions.**

1. Which pictures show problems with supplies?
2. Which pictures show problems with equipment?

Practice

A 🔘 80 **Listen to the conversation. Listen again and repeat.**

A: What's the problem?
B: The oven isn't working.
A: Tell your supervisor.

B *PAIRS.* **Practice the conversation. Use other problems in Learn.**

Make It Yours

A *PAIRS.* **Brainstorm other problems at work.**

Equipment   Supplies

_____   _____.
_____ } isn't working. We're out of { _____.
_____   _____.
_____   _____.

B **Write a new conversation like the one in Practice.**

C **Role-play your conversation for the class.**

BONUS *GROUPS OF 3.* **Tell about a real problem you had at work with equipment or supplies.**

_____
_____
_____
_____

Unit 12 Test

Before you take the test

A B C D | Use the answer sheet for Unit 12 on page 227.

1. Print your name.
2. Print your teacher's name.
3. Write your student identification number, and bubble in the information below the boxes.
4. Write the test date and bubble in the information.
5. Write your class number and bubble in the information.

Listening I [Tracks 81–85]

Look at the pictures and listen. What is the correct answer: A, B, or C?

1.

A

B

C

2.

A

B

C

3.

Grandpa's Restaurant

Waiters full time

Must have experience

M-F 6:00 A.M.–2:00 P.M.

Apply in person

A

Metro Hotel
P/T housekeeper
Exp. req.
Apply online at
metrohotel@city.com
or call 234-555-9876

B

Dante's Pizza

F/T delivery person

12:00–8:00

Driver's lic. req.

Apply in person

C

4.

A

B

C

Listening II [Tracks 86–89]

Listen. Everything is on the audio CD.

Reading

Read. What is the correct answer: A, B, C, or D?

8. What does she do?

    A. She's a cook.

    B. She's a bus driver.

    C. She's an office clerk.

    D. She's a painter.

9. What does a construction worker do?

    A. prepares food

    B. builds houses

    C. fixes sinks and toilets

    D. answers the phone and uses the computer

City Diner

Cashiers Needed

F/T M–F 12:00–7:00

No exp. req. Will train.

Apply in person.

10. How can you apply for this job?

    A. It's four days a week.

    B. You should go to City Diner.

    C. You should apply online.

    D. You don't need experience.

11. What was your last job?

    A. I was a gardener for ten years.

    B. I was a cook last year.

    C. I worked Monday to Friday.

    D. It was a part-time job.

12. What does the woman answer?

    A. No, I can't, but I can learn.

    B. Can you use a cash register?

    C. I've been an office assistant for three years.

    D. I'm not a gardener.

$AVEMORE MARKET

WORK SCHEDULE

Name	Task	Days	Times
① Garcia, Jose	stock clerk	Mon.–Fri.	2:00 to 8:00 P.M.
② Wu, Ming	cashier	Wed.–Sun.	8:00 A.M. to 4:00 P.M.
③ Busseret, Pierre	custodian	Sat.	4:00 to 8:00 P.M.
④ Kasakov, Yuri	cashier	Mon.–Tues.	8:00 A.M. to 4:00 P.M.

13. His days off are Monday and Tuesday.

    A. ①

    B. ②

    C. ③

    D. ④

14. What's the problem?

    A. The cash register isn't working.

    B. The oven isn't working.

    C. Tell your supervisor.

    D. We're out of detergent.

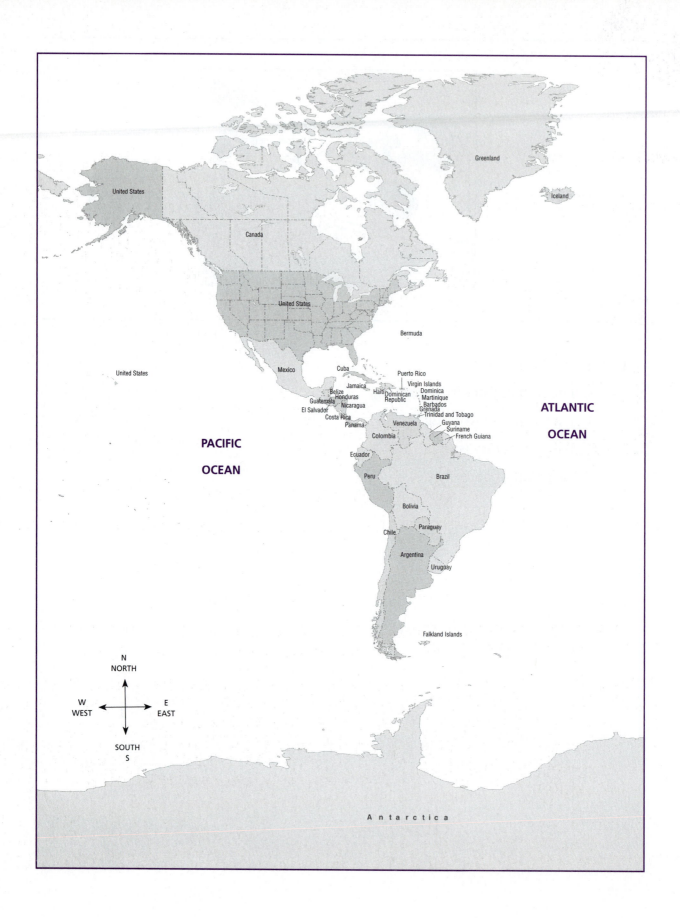

Greenland

Iceland

United States

Canada

United States

United States

Mexico

Bermuda

Cuba

Jamaica

Puerto Rico

Virgin Islands

Belize
Honduras

Haiti

Dominican
Republic

Dominica
Martinique
Barbados

Guatemala

Nicaragua

Grenada

El Salvador

Trinidad and Tobago

Costa Rica

Panama

Venezuela

Guyana

Colombia

Suriname
French Guiana

ATLANTIC

OCEAN

Ecuador

PACIFIC

OCEAN

Peru

Brazil

Bolivia

Paraguay

Chile

Argentina

Uruguay

Falkland Islands

N
NORTH

W
WEST

E
EAST

SOUTH
S

A n t a r c t i c a

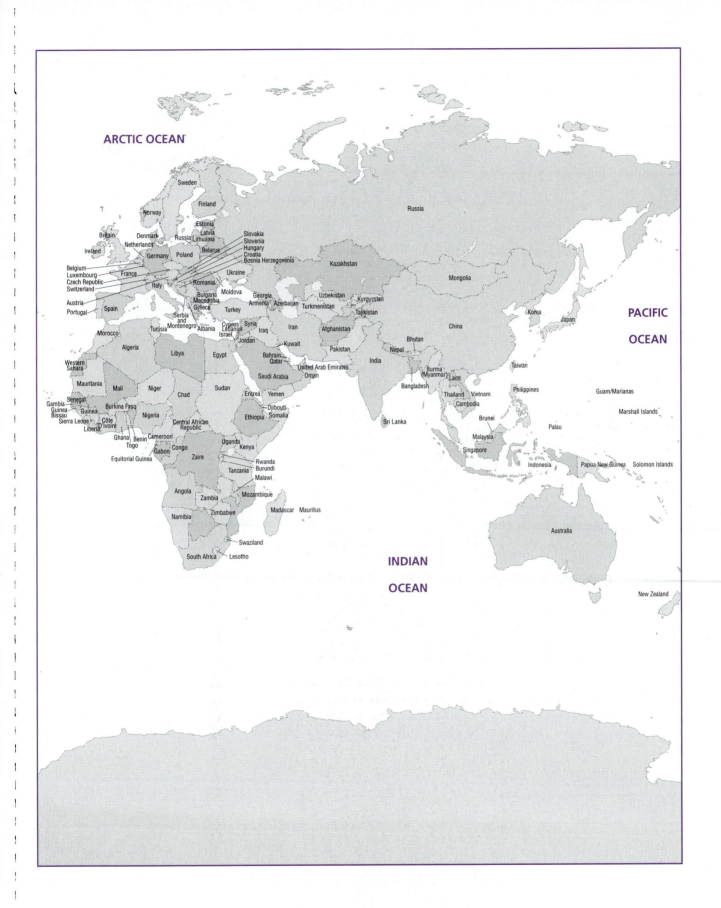

ARCTIC OCEAN

Sweden

Finland

Norway

Russia

Britain
Denmark
Netherlands
Ireland
Germany Poland
Belgium
Luxembourg France
Czech Republic
Switzerland Italy
Austria
Portugal Spain

Estonia
Latvia
Russia Lithuania
Belarus

Slovakia
Slovenia
Hungary
Croatia
Bosnia Herzegovenia

Ukraine

Kazakhstan

Mongolia

Romania
Bulgaria
Macedonia
Greece
Serbia
and
Montenegro Albania
Tunisia
Morocco

Moldova
Georgia
Armenia Azerbaijan
Turkey
Cyprus Syria
Lebanon
Israel
Jordan

Uzbekistan
Kyrgyzstan
Turkmenistan
Tajikistan

Korea
Japan

PACIFIC

OCEAN

Iran
Afghanistan

China

Algeria
Libya
Egypt

Iraq
Kuwait

Pakistan

Bhutan
Nepal

Taiwan

Western
Sahara

Mauritania
Mali
Niger
Chad
Sudan

Bahrain
Qatar
United Arab Emirates
Oman

Saudi Arabia

India

Burma
(Myanmar) Laos

Bangladesh

Philippines

Guam/Marianas

Marshall Islands

Eritrea Yemen
Gambia
Guinea
Bissau Senegal
Sierra Leone Guinea
Liberia Côte
D'Ivoire
Burkina Faso
Nigeria
Ghana Benin Cameroon
Togo
Gabon Congo
Equitorial Guinea

Central African
Republic

Djibouti
Ethiopia Somalia

Thailand Vietnam
Cambodia

Brunei

Sri Lanka

Malaysia

Palau

Singapore

Uganda
Kenya

Indonesia

Papua New Guinea

Solomon Islands

Zaire
Angola
Zambia
Namibia

Rwanda
Burundi
Tanzania
Malawi

Mozambique
Zimbabwe

Madascar Mauritus

Australia

Swaziland
South Africa Lesotho

INDIAN

OCEAN

New Zealand

197

Alaska

Saint
Lawrence
Island

Patrick Island

Ellesmere
Island

Axel
Heiberg
Island

Sverdrup Islands

Queen Elizabeth Islands

Banks
Island

Melville
Island

Devon Island

Kodiak
Island

Prince
of
Wales
Island

Victoria Island

Baffin Island

Yukon
Territory

Northwest
Territories

Nunavut

Queen
Charlotte
Islands

British
Columbia

Alberta

Saskatchewan

Manitoba

Vancouver Island

C A N A D A

Ontario

Quebec

Newfoundland

Newfoundland

Washington

Montana

North Dakota

Minnesota

New
Brunswick

Prince
Edward
Island

Oregon

Idaho

South Dakota

Wisconsin

Michigan

Ottawa

Vermont

Maine

Nova Scotia

New Hampshire

Nevada

Wyoming

U. S. A.

Iowa

Illinois

Indiana

Ohio

New York

Massachusetts

Rhode Island
Connecticut

Pennsylvania

New Jersey

California

Utah

Colorado

Nebraska

Kansas

Missouri

West
Virginia

Virginia

Delaware
Maryland
Washington D. C.

Arizona

New Mexico

Oklahoma

Kentucky

Tennessee

North Carolina

Arkansas

Texas

Alabama

Georgia

South
Carolina

Mississippi

Louisiana

Florida

Hawaii

Puerto Rico

○ = state, province, or territory capital
◉ = country capital

United States Postal Abbreviations

Alabama	AL	Louisiana	LA	Ohio	OH
Alaska	AK	Maine	ME	Oklahoma	OK
Arizona	AZ	Maryland	MD	Oregon	OR
Arkansas	AR	Massachusetts	MA	Pennsylvania	PA
California	CA	Michigan	MI	Puerto Rico	PR
Colorado	CO	Minnesota	MN	Rhode Island	RI
Connecticut	CT	Mississippi	MS	South Carolina	SC
Delaware	DE	Missouri	MO	South Dakota	SD
District of Columbia	DC	Montana	MT	Tennessee	TN
Florida	FL	Nebraska	NE	Texas	TX
Georgia	GA	Nevada	NV	Utah	UT
Hawaii	HI	New Hampshire	NH	Vermont	VT
Idaho	ID	New Jersey	NJ	Virginia	VA
Illinois	IL	New Mexico	NM	Washington	WA
Indiana	IN	New York	NY	West Virginia	WV
Iowa	IA	North Carolina	NC	Wisconsin	WI
Kansas	KS	North Dakota	ND	Wyoming	WY
Kentucky	KY				

Canadian Postal Abbreviations

Alberta	AB	Newfoundland and Labrador	NL	Prince Edward Island	PE
British Columbia	BC	Northwest Territories	NT	Quebec	QC
Manitoba	MB	Nova Scotia	NS	Saskatchewan	SK
New Brunswick	NB	Nunavut	NU	Yukon	YT

United States Capitals

Alabama	Montgomery	Louisiana	Baton Rouge	Ohio	Columbus
Alaska	Juneau	Maine	Augusta	Oklahoma	Oklahoma City
Arizona	Phoenix	Maryland	Annapolis	Oregon	Salem
Arkansas	Little Rock	Massachusetts	Boston	Pennsylvania	Harrisburg
California	Sacramento	Michigan	Lansing	Rhode Island	Providence
Colorado	Denver	Minnesota	Saint Paul	South Carolina	Columbia
Connecticut	Hartford	Mississippi	Jackson	South Dakota	Pierre
Delaware	Dover	Missouri	Jefferson City	Tennessee	Nashville
Florida	Tallahassee	Montana	Helena	Texas	Austin
Georgia	Atlanta	Nebraska	Lincoln	Utah	Salt Lake City
Hawaii	Honolulu	Nevada	Carson City	Vermont	Montpelier
Idaho	Boise	New Hampshire	Concord	Virginia	Richmond
Illinois	Springfield	New Jersey	Trenton	Washington	Olympia
Indiana	Indianapolis	New Mexico	Santa Fe	West Virginia	Charleston
Iowa	Des Moines	New York	Albany	Wisconsin	Madison
Kansas	Topeka	North Carolina	Raleigh	Wyoming	Cheyenne
Kentucky	Frankfort	North Dakota	Bismarck		

Canadian Capitals

Alberta	Edmonton	Nova Scotia	Halifax
British Columbia	Victoria	Nunavut	Iqaluit
Manitoba	Winnipeg	Prince Edward Island	Charlottetown
New Brunswick	Fredericton	Quebec	Quebec City
Newfoundland and Labrador	St. John's	Saskatchewan	Regina
Northwest Territories	Yellowknife	Yukon	Whitehorse

Audioscript

Unit 1 Lesson 3

Practice, Exercise C page 7

1. Mr. Lee
2. Ms. Thompson
3. Miss Roberts
4. Mr. Sanchez
5. Mrs. Sanchez, Ms. Sanchez

Lesson 4

Listen page 9

1.
A: Who's that?
B: That's my brother.

2.
A: This is my daughter. Her name is Ella.

3.
A: Who's that?
B: That's my son. His name is Juan.

4.
A: Is that your father?
B: Yes. His name is Frank.

5.
A: This is my wife. Her name is Mi Kyung.

6.
A: Who's that?
B: That's my husband.

Lesson 5

Learn, Exercise A pages 10–11

Canada   China
The United States   Korea
Mexico   Senegal
Ecuador   Somalia
Russia   Vietnam
Spain

Listen page 12

1.
A: Where are you from?
B: I'm from Russia.

2.
A: Where are you from?
B: I'm from Mexico.

3.
A: Where is Mai from?
B: She's from Vietnam.

4.
A: Where is Paul from?
B: He's from Senegal.

Unit 2 Lesson 1

Learn, Exercise B page 18

1. D	7. N
2. X	8. L
3. G	9. E
4. F	10. V
5. S	11. O
6. P	12. T

Practice, Exercise B page 18

1. Name. N-A-M-E. Name.
2. Nice. N-I-C-E. Nice.
3. Last. L-A-S-T. Last.
4. Meet. M-E-E-T. Meet.
5. Hello. H-E-L-L-O. Hello.
6. First. F-I-R-S-T. First.

Lesson 2

Practice, Exercise B page 20

1. 212-288-0594
   (two one two-two eight eight-oh five nine four)
2. 718-499-2805
3. 407-328-4722
4. 617-969-0387
5. 916-492-1925
6. 802-254-3431

Lesson 4

Listen page 23

1.
A: What's your address?
B: 9516 North Beach Avenue.

2.
A: What's your address?
B: 227 West New York Street.

3.
A: What's your address?
B: 320 Tall Oaks Drive.

4.
A: What's your address?
B: 1306 Hudson Boulevard.

5.
A: What's your address?
B: 185 Park Avenue Northwest.

Unit 3 Lesson 1

Learn, **Exercise B** page 36

1. Write in your notebook.
2. Raise your hand.
3. Take out a pen.
4. Open your book.
5. Put away your dictionary.
6. Copy the sentence.
7. Close your book.
8. Look at the board.

Practice, **Exercise B** page 37

1. b. Take out a pen.
2. c. Write on the board.
3. d. Close your book.
4. a. Raise your hand.
5. f. Copy the word.
6. e. Put away your pencil.

Lesson 2

Learn, **Exercise C** page 39

1. The library is across from the office.
2. The office is next to Room 102.
3. The computer lab is across from the student lounge.
4. The men's room is next to the computer lab.
5. The ladies' room is across from the men's room.
6. The stairs are next to the ladies' room.

Lesson 4

Listen page 42

1. fifteenth
2. seventy-seventh
3. fortieth
4. thirty-third
5. eighty-eighth
6. ninety-first

Lesson 5

Learn page 43

1. principal
2. teacher
3. security guard
4. custodian
5. receptionist
6. student

Unit 4 Lesson 1

Learn, **Exercise A** page 50

It's one o'clock.
It's two-oh-five.
It's three ten.
It's four fifteen.
It's five twenty.
It's six twenty-five.
It's seven thirty.
It's eight thirty-five.
It's nine forty.
It's ten forty-five.
It's eleven fifty.
It's twelve fifty-five.

Listen page 51

1.
A: What time is it?
B: It's twelve.

2.
A: What time is it?
B: It's ten o'clock.

3.
A: What time is it?
B: It's one thirty.

4.
A: What time is it?
B: It's three forty-five.

Lesson 2

Listen page 53

1.
A: What day is today?
B: It's Saturday.

2.
A: When is ESL 4?
B: It's on Tuesday and Thursday.

3.
A: When is your class?
B: It's on Monday, Wednesday, and Friday.

Lesson 4

Learn page 57

August tenth, two thousand seven
March thirty-first, nineteen ninety-nine
April ninth, two thousand four
December twelfth, two thousand five

Practice, **Exercise A** page 57

1. January 15th, 2005
2. December 2nd, 2001
3. February 10th, 1997
4. November 11th, 1911
5. March 5th, 1955
6. October 16th, 1968
7. April 19th, 1977
8. September 23rd, 1988
9. May 30th, 2000
10. August 20th, 1994
11. July 21st, 1990
12. June 14th, 2003

Lesson 7

Learn, **Exercise B** page 61

1. windy
2. hot
3. rainy
4. warm
5. cold
6. snowy
7. sunny
8. cool
9. cloudy

Learn, Exercise A page 62

It's ninety degrees Fahrenheit.
It's seventy degrees Fahrenheit.
It's fifty degrees Fahrenheit.
It's thirty degrees Fahrenheit.

Practice page 63

1. It's sunny and cool in San Francisco. It's sixty degrees.
2. It's cloudy and warm in Los Angeles. It's seventy-five degrees.
3. It's rainy and cool in Seattle. It's fifty degrees.
4. It's windy and cold in Chicago. It's twenty degrees.
5. It's sunny and hot in Miami. It's eighty degrees.
6. It's snowy and cold in Boston. It's thirty degrees.

Unit 5 Lesson 1

Learn, Exercise B page 72

1.
A: Where are you?
B: I'm at the supermarket.

2.
A: Where are you?
B: I'm at the bank.

3.
A: Where is Matt?
B: He's at the post office.

4.
A: Where is Charlene?
B: She's at the drugstore.

5.
A: Where are Stacey and Elaine?
B: They're at the library.

Learn, Exercise A page 73

1. The post office is on First Street.
2. The drugstore is on Oak Street.
3. The supermarket is on Main Street.

Lesson 2

Learn, Exercise B page 74

1. walk
2. ride a bike
3. take the train
4. drive a car
5. take the subway
6. carpool in a van
7. ride a motorcycle
8. take the bus

Listen page 75

1.
A: How do you get to work?
B: I take the bus.

2.
A: Do you drive to work?
B: No, I ride my bike.

3.
A: Where's your car?
B: It's over there.

4.
A: How do you get to school?
B: I drive.

5.
A: How many people are in your carpool?
B: Four.

Lesson 3

Learn page 76

Bus number 15 goes to First Street.
Bus number 604 goes to City Center.
Bus number 18 goes downtown.
Bus number 10 goes to Broadway.

Learn page 76

The G train goes to Forest Hills.
The A train goes to Rockaway.
The N train goes to Astoria.
The S train goes to Times Square.

Lesson 5

Learn, Exercise B page 79

1. stop
2. one way only
3. school crossing
4. no parking
5. railroad crossing
6. do not enter

Unit 6 Lesson 1

Learn, Exercise A page 88

1. a dollar
2. five dollars
3. ten dollars
4. twenty dollars

Learn, Exercise E page 88

1. b. a nickel
2. c. a dime
3. d. a quarter
4. a. a penny

Learn, Exercise A page 90

$2.99
$43.25
$58.00
$79.03
$110.50

Listen page 91

1. five dollars
2. a quarter
3. A dime is ten cents.
4. thirty-four ninety-nine

5.
A: Do you have change for a dollar?
B: No, I'm sorry. I don't.

6.
A: How much money do you have?
B: One hundred fifty dollars.

Lesson 5

Learn page 97

thirty-six ninety-nine
twenty-five dollars
ten ninety-nine
twenty-two dollars

twelve ninety-nine
thirty ninety-nine
fifty-nine ninety-nine
nineteen dollars

Unit 7 Lesson 3

Learn, Exercise A page 110

two ninety-nine each
one ninety-nine a quart
ninety-nine cents a dozen

ninety-nine cents a gallon
two ninety-nine a pound
three ninety-nine a half-gallon

Lesson 4

Learn, Exercise A page 112

a hamburger
a hot dog
a pizza
a taco
a sandwich
a salad
fries
frozen yogurt

apple pie
ice cream
coffee
iced tea
soda
milk
juice

Listen page 113

1. I'd like a hot dog, please.
2. I'd like ice cream, please.
3. I'd like coffee, please.
4. I'd like a salad, please.

Unit 8 Lesson 2

Learn, Exercise A page 122

refrigerator
microwave
sink
dishwasher
stove

shower
sink
toilet
bathtub

Listen page 124

1. Marc is in the bedroom.
2. The dresser is across from the bed.
3. The soup is on the stove.
4. The microwave is new.

Unit 9 Lesson 2

Learn, Exercise A page 138

A: Metro Adult School. This is Ms. Sanchez.
B: Hello. May I speak to Ms. Grover?
A: I'm sorry. She's not here right now. Can I take a message?
B: Yes. Please have her call Marta Gomez at 718-555-3499.
A: I'll give her the message. Thank you for calling. Good-bye.

A: Metro Business Machines. This is Edgar.
B: Hello. Is Mr. Pacer there?
A: I'm sorry. He's not in. May I take your name and number?
B: Yes. My name is Bob Carey and my number is 212-555-8541.
A: I'll give him the message. Thank you for calling. Good-bye.

A: Dr. Sanders's office. This is Kristina.
B: Hello. May I speak to Dr. Sanders?
A: I'm sorry. She's not available. Can I have her call you?
B: Yes. My name is Ming Tan. My number is 802-555-6789.
A: I'll give her the message. Thank you for calling. Good-bye.

Lesson 3

Learn, Exercise B page 140

1.
A: Metro Department Store.
B: Hi. This is Pedro. I'm going to be late. I have a flat tire. Please tell Mr. Tran.
A: OK, I'll give him the message.

2.
A: Metro Water Company.
B: Hi. This is Lynda Yu. I can't come to work today. My mother is in the hospital. Please tell Ms. Sutton.
A: OK, I'll give her the message.

3.
A: Metro Garbage Company.
B: Hi. This is Mark Feldman. I can't come to work today. My son is sick. Please tell Chico.
A: OK, I'll give him the message.

4.

A: Big Business Company.

B: Hi. This is Rita. I can't come to work today. I'm sick. Please tell Mrs. Haines.

A: OK, I'll give her the message.

5.

A: Metro Community Hospital.

B: Hi. This is George Choi. I'm going to be late. There's a lot of traffic. Please tell Dr. Salinas.

A: OK, I'll give her the message.

6.

A: Metro Mini Mart.

B: Hi. This is Maria Irizarry. I can't come to work today. I had an accident. Please tell Gus.

A: OK, I'll give him the message.

Listen page 141

1. Hi. This is Jack Mayer. I'm going to be late. I have a flat tire.
2. Hello, Sophie? This is Patty Baker. I'm going to be absent today. My mother is in the hospital.
3. Hi, Tom. This is Amanda. I'm not coming to work today. I had a car accident. Please tell Mr. Price.

Unit 10 Lesson 2

Learn, Exercise B page 150

1. d. I have a headache.
2. c. I have an earache.
3. a. I have a toothache.
4. e. I have a backache.
5. b. I have a stomachache.

Learn, Exercise F page 151

1. I have the flu.
2. I have a cold.
3. I have a sore throat.
4. I have a fever.
5. I have a cough.

Listen page 153

1. My stomach hurts.
2. I have a toothache.
3. I have a backache.

Lesson 3

Learn, Exercise B page 155

Your next appointment is on Monday, June 22nd, at 11:30.

Your next appointment is on Friday, March 10th, at 9 o'clock.

Your next appointment is on Wednesday, November 18th, at 4 o'clock.

Make It Yours, Exercise B page 156

1. Your next appointment is on Tuesday, February third, at noon.
2. Your next appointment is on Thursday, August thirteenth, at 3 o'clock.

Listen page 156

1. Your next appointment is on Thursday, June fourth, at two P.M.
2. Your next appointment is on Monday, May thirteenth, at ten thirty.
3. Your next appointment is on Friday, October tenth, at two o'clock.

Unit 11 Lesson 1

Learn, Exercise A page 164

a. Danger!
b. Caution: wet floor
c. No smoking
d. Do not enter
e. Exit
f. No parking

Lesson 2

Listen page 166

1. Walk!
2. Wait!
3. Watch out!
4. Don't touch!

Unit 12 Lesson 2

Listen page 179

1. He serves food and drinks.
2. She cleans hotel rooms and makes beds.
3. He gives legal help and goes to court.
4. She builds houses.
5. She sells clothes.

Lesson 5

Learn, Exercise A page 183

Tom Brady works Wednesday to Saturday from 9 to 1.

Maria Gomez works Sunday, Monday, Tuesday, and Thursday, from 12 to 8:30.

Lin Nam works Monday to Friday from 1 to 5.

Ricardo Perez works Saturday and Sunday from 8 to 4.

Lesson 5

Listen page 184

Mark Albers works Monday, Tuesday, Friday, and Saturday from 11 to 3.

Sue Bart works Tuesday to Saturday from 9 to 5.

Sonya Lopez works Thursday to Monday from 5 to 10.

Lin Tran works Wednesday to Sunday from 1 to 5.

Lesson 6

Learn page 186

1. We're out of paper.
2. We're out of sugar.
3. We're out of detergent.
4. The oven isn't working.
5. The computer isn't working.
6. The cash register isn't working.

Life Skills and Test Prep 1
Unit 1 Test Answer Sheet

① _____
  Last Name   First Name   Middle

② _____
  Teacher's Name

TEST

1 Ⓐ Ⓑ Ⓒ Ⓓ
2 Ⓐ Ⓑ Ⓒ Ⓓ
3 Ⓐ Ⓑ Ⓒ Ⓓ
4 Ⓐ Ⓑ Ⓒ Ⓓ
5 Ⓐ Ⓑ Ⓒ Ⓓ
6 Ⓐ Ⓑ Ⓒ Ⓓ
7 Ⓐ Ⓑ Ⓒ Ⓓ
8 Ⓐ Ⓑ Ⓒ Ⓓ
9 Ⓐ Ⓑ Ⓒ Ⓓ
10 Ⓐ Ⓑ Ⓒ Ⓓ
11 Ⓐ Ⓑ Ⓒ Ⓓ
12 Ⓐ Ⓑ Ⓒ Ⓓ
13 Ⓐ Ⓑ Ⓒ Ⓓ
14 Ⓐ Ⓑ Ⓒ Ⓓ
15 Ⓐ Ⓑ Ⓒ Ⓓ
16 Ⓐ Ⓑ Ⓒ Ⓓ
17 Ⓐ Ⓑ Ⓒ Ⓓ
18 Ⓐ Ⓑ Ⓒ Ⓓ
19 Ⓐ Ⓑ Ⓒ Ⓓ
20 Ⓐ Ⓑ Ⓒ Ⓓ

Directions for marking answers

- Use a No. 2 pencil. Do NOT use ink.
- Make dark marks and bubble in your answers completely.
- If you change an answer, erase your first mark completely.

Right
Ⓐ Ⓑ Ⓒ Ⓓ

Wrong
Ⓐ Ⓧ Ⓒ Ⓓ
Ⓐ Ⓑ Ⓒ Ⓓ

③ STUDENT IDENTIFICATION

(number bubble grid 0–9, nine columns)

Is this your Social Security number?
Yes ◯   No ◯

④ TEST DATE

MM	D	D	Y	Y
Jan	0	0	200	0
Feb	1	1	200	1
Mar	2	2	200	2
Apr	3	3	200	3
May		4	200	4
Jun		5	200	5
Jul		6	200	6
Aug		7	200	7
Sep		8	200	8
Oct		9	200	9
Nov				
Dec				

⑤ CLASS NUMBER

(number bubble grid 0–9, eight columns)

⑥ RAW SCORE

(number bubble grid 0–9, two columns)

Life Skills and Test Prep 1
Unit 1 Test Answer Sheet

① _____

    Last Name   First Name   Middle

② _____

    Teacher's Name

TEST

1 Ⓐ Ⓑ Ⓒ Ⓓ

2 Ⓐ Ⓑ Ⓒ Ⓓ

3 Ⓐ Ⓑ Ⓒ Ⓓ

4 Ⓐ Ⓑ Ⓒ Ⓓ

5 Ⓐ Ⓑ Ⓒ Ⓓ

6 Ⓐ Ⓑ Ⓒ Ⓓ

7 Ⓐ Ⓑ Ⓒ Ⓓ

8 Ⓐ Ⓑ Ⓒ Ⓓ

9 Ⓐ Ⓑ Ⓒ Ⓓ

10 Ⓐ Ⓑ Ⓒ Ⓓ

11 Ⓐ Ⓑ Ⓒ Ⓓ

12 Ⓐ Ⓑ Ⓒ Ⓓ

13 Ⓐ Ⓑ Ⓒ Ⓓ

14 Ⓐ Ⓑ Ⓒ Ⓓ

15 Ⓐ Ⓑ Ⓒ Ⓓ

16 Ⓐ Ⓑ Ⓒ Ⓓ

17 Ⓐ Ⓑ Ⓒ Ⓓ

18 Ⓐ Ⓑ Ⓒ Ⓓ

19 Ⓐ Ⓑ Ⓒ Ⓓ

20 Ⓐ Ⓑ Ⓒ Ⓓ

Directions for marking answers

- Use a No. 2 pencil. Do NOT use ink.
- Make dark marks and bubble in your answers completely.
- If you change an answer, erase your first mark completely.

Right

Ⓐ ⬤ Ⓒ Ⓓ

Wrong

Ⓐ ⊗ Ⓒ Ⓓ

Ⓐ Ⓑ Ⓒ Ⓓ

③ STUDENT IDENTIFICATION

0	0	0		0	0		0	0	0
1	1	1		1	1		1	1	1
2	2	2		2	2		2	2	2
3	3	3		3	3		3	3	3
4	4	4		4	4		4	4	4
5	5	5		5	5		5	5	5
6	6	6		6	6		6	6	6
7	7	7		7	7		7	7	7
8	8	8		8	8		8	8	8
9	9	9		9	9		9	9	9

Is this your Social Security number?

Yes ⬭   No ⬭

④ TEST DATE

MM	D	D	Y	Y
Jan ⬭	0	0	200	0
Feb ⬭	1	1	200	1
Mar ⬭	2	2	200	2
Apr ⬭	3	3	200	3
May ⬭		4	200	4
Jun ⬭		5	200	5
Jul ⬭		6	200	6
Aug ⬭		7	200	7
Sep ⬭		8	200	8
Oct ⬭		9	200	9
Nov ⬭				
Dec ⬭				

⑤ CLASS NUMBER

0	0	0	0	0	0	0	0
1	1	1	1	1	1	1	1
2	2	2	2	2	2	2	2
3	3	3	3	3	3	3	3
4	4	4	4	4	4	4	4
5	5	5	5	5	5	5	5
6	6	6	6	6	6	6	6
7	7	7	7	7	7	7	7
8	8	8	8	8	8	8	8
9	9	9	9	9	9	9	9

⑥ RAW SCORE

0	0
1	1
2	2
3	3
4	4
5	5
6	6
7	7
8	8
9	9

Life Skills and Test Prep 1
Unit 2 Test Answer Sheet

① _____

Last Name   First Name   Middle

② _____

Teacher's Name

TEST

1 Ⓐ Ⓑ Ⓒ Ⓓ
2 Ⓐ Ⓑ Ⓒ Ⓓ
3 Ⓐ Ⓑ Ⓒ Ⓓ
4 Ⓐ Ⓑ Ⓒ Ⓓ
5 Ⓐ Ⓑ Ⓒ Ⓓ
6 Ⓐ Ⓑ Ⓒ Ⓓ
7 Ⓐ Ⓑ Ⓒ Ⓓ
8 Ⓐ Ⓑ Ⓒ Ⓓ
9 Ⓐ Ⓑ Ⓒ Ⓓ
10 Ⓐ Ⓑ Ⓒ Ⓓ
11 Ⓐ Ⓑ Ⓒ Ⓓ
12 Ⓐ Ⓑ Ⓒ Ⓓ
13 Ⓐ Ⓑ Ⓒ Ⓓ
14 Ⓐ Ⓑ Ⓒ Ⓓ
15 Ⓐ Ⓑ Ⓒ Ⓓ
16 Ⓐ Ⓑ Ⓒ Ⓓ
17 Ⓐ Ⓑ Ⓒ Ⓓ
18 Ⓐ Ⓑ Ⓒ Ⓓ
19 Ⓐ Ⓑ Ⓒ Ⓓ
20 Ⓐ Ⓑ Ⓒ Ⓓ

Directions for marking answers

- Use a No. 2 pencil. Do NOT use ink.
- Make dark marks and bubble in your answers completely.
- If you change an answer, erase your first mark completely.

Right

Ⓐ ⬤Ⓑ Ⓒ Ⓓ

Wrong

Ⓐ ⊗ Ⓒ Ⓓ
Ⓐ Ⓑ Ⓒ Ⓓ

③ STUDENT IDENTIFICATION

Is this your Social Security number?

Yes ☐   No ☐

④ TEST DATE

MM	D	D	Y	Y
Jan	0	0	200	0
Feb	1	1	200	1
Mar	2	2	200	2
Apr	3	3	200	3
May		4	200	4
Jun		5	200	5
Jul		6	200	6
Aug		7	200	7
Sep		8	200	8
Oct		9	200	9
Nov				
Dec				

⑤ CLASS NUMBER

⑥ RAW SCORE

Life Skills and Test Prep 1
Unit 2 Test Answer Sheet

① _____

    Last Name   First Name   Middle

② _____

    Teacher's Name

TEST

1 Ⓐ Ⓑ Ⓒ Ⓓ
2 Ⓐ Ⓑ Ⓒ Ⓓ
3 Ⓐ Ⓑ Ⓒ Ⓓ
4 Ⓐ Ⓑ Ⓒ Ⓓ
5 Ⓐ Ⓑ Ⓒ Ⓓ
6 Ⓐ Ⓑ Ⓒ Ⓓ
7 Ⓐ Ⓑ Ⓒ Ⓓ
8 Ⓐ Ⓑ Ⓒ Ⓓ
9 Ⓐ Ⓑ Ⓒ Ⓓ
10 Ⓐ Ⓑ Ⓒ Ⓓ
11 Ⓐ Ⓑ Ⓒ Ⓓ
12 Ⓐ Ⓑ Ⓒ Ⓓ
13 Ⓐ Ⓑ Ⓒ Ⓓ
14 Ⓐ Ⓑ Ⓒ Ⓓ
15 Ⓐ Ⓑ Ⓒ Ⓓ
16 Ⓐ Ⓑ Ⓒ Ⓓ
17 Ⓐ Ⓑ Ⓒ Ⓓ
18 Ⓐ Ⓑ Ⓒ Ⓓ
19 Ⓐ Ⓑ Ⓒ Ⓓ
20 Ⓐ Ⓑ Ⓒ Ⓓ

Directions for marking answers

- Use a No. 2 pencil. Do NOT use ink.
- Make dark marks and bubble in your answers completely.
- If you change an answer, erase your first mark completely.

Right
Ⓐ ● Ⓒ Ⓓ

Wrong
Ⓐ ⊠ Ⓒ Ⓓ
Ⓐ Ⓑ Ⓒ Ⓓ

③ **STUDENT IDENTIFICATION**

Is this your Social Security number?
Yes ◯ No ◯

④ **TEST DATE**

MM	D	D	Y	Y

Jan, Feb, Mar, Apr, May, Jun, Jul, Aug, Sep, Oct, Nov, Dec

⑤ **CLASS NUMBER**

⑥ **RAW SCORE**

Life Skills and Test Prep 1
Unit 3 Test Answer Sheet

① _____
Last Name   First Name   Middle

② _____
Teacher's Name

TEST

1 Ⓐ Ⓑ Ⓒ Ⓓ
2 Ⓐ Ⓑ Ⓒ Ⓓ
3 Ⓐ Ⓑ Ⓒ Ⓓ
4 Ⓐ Ⓑ Ⓒ Ⓓ
5 Ⓐ Ⓑ Ⓒ Ⓓ
6 Ⓐ Ⓑ Ⓒ Ⓓ
7 Ⓐ Ⓑ Ⓒ Ⓓ
8 Ⓐ Ⓑ Ⓒ Ⓓ
9 Ⓐ Ⓑ Ⓒ Ⓓ
10 Ⓐ Ⓑ Ⓒ Ⓓ
11 Ⓐ Ⓑ Ⓒ Ⓓ
12 Ⓐ Ⓑ Ⓒ Ⓓ
13 Ⓐ Ⓑ Ⓒ Ⓓ
14 Ⓐ Ⓑ Ⓒ Ⓓ
15 Ⓐ Ⓑ Ⓒ Ⓓ
16 Ⓐ Ⓑ Ⓒ Ⓓ
17 Ⓐ Ⓑ Ⓒ Ⓓ
18 Ⓐ Ⓑ Ⓒ Ⓓ
19 Ⓐ Ⓑ Ⓒ Ⓓ
20 Ⓐ Ⓑ Ⓒ Ⓓ

Directions for marking answers

- Use a No. 2 pencil. Do NOT use ink.
- Make dark marks and bubble in your answers completely.
- If you change an answer, erase your first mark completely.

Right
Ⓐ ● Ⓒ Ⓓ

Wrong
Ⓐ ⊗ Ⓒ Ⓓ
Ⓐ Ⓑ Ⓒ Ⓓ

③ STUDENT IDENTIFICATION

⓪	⓪	⓪	⓪	⓪	⓪	⓪	⓪	⓪
①	①	①	①	①	①	①	①	①
②	②	②	②	②	②	②	②	②
③	③	③	③	③	③	③	③	③
④	④	④	④	④	④	④	④	④
⑤	⑤	⑤	⑤	⑤	⑤	⑤	⑤	⑤
⑥	⑥	⑥	⑥	⑥	⑥	⑥	⑥	⑥
⑦	⑦	⑦	⑦	⑦	⑦	⑦	⑦	⑦
⑧	⑧	⑧	⑧	⑧	⑧	⑧	⑧	⑧
⑨	⑨	⑨	⑨	⑨	⑨	⑨	⑨	⑨

Is this your Social Security number?
Yes ☐   No ☐

④ TEST DATE

MM	D	D		Y	Y
Jan ☐	⓪	⓪	200		⓪
Feb ☐	①	①	200		①
Mar ☐	②	②	200		②
Apr ☐	③	③	200		③
May ☐		④	200		④
Jun ☐		⑤	200		⑤
Jul ☐		⑥	200		⑥
Aug ☐		⑦	200		⑦
Sep ☐		⑧	200		⑧
Oct ☐		⑨	200		⑨
Nov ☐					
Dec ☐					

⑤ CLASS NUMBER

⓪	⓪	⓪	⓪	⓪	⓪	⓪	⓪
①	①	①	①	①	①	①	①
②	②	②	②	②	②	②	②
③	③	③	③	③	③	③	③
④	④	④	④	④	④	④	④
⑤	⑤	⑤	⑤	⑤	⑤	⑤	⑤
⑥	⑥	⑥	⑥	⑥	⑥	⑥	⑥
⑦	⑦	⑦	⑦	⑦	⑦	⑦	⑦
⑧	⑧	⑧	⑧	⑧	⑧	⑧	⑧
⑨	⑨	⑨	⑨	⑨	⑨	⑨	⑨

⑥ RAW SCORE

⓪	⓪
①	①
②	②
③	③
④	④
⑤	⑤
⑥	⑥
⑦	⑦
⑧	⑧
⑨	⑨

Life Skills and Test Prep 1
Unit 3 Test Answer Sheet

① _____

Last Name   First Name   Middle

② _____

Teacher's Name

TEST

1 Ⓐ Ⓑ Ⓒ Ⓓ
2 Ⓐ Ⓑ Ⓒ Ⓓ
3 Ⓐ Ⓑ Ⓒ Ⓓ
4 Ⓐ Ⓑ Ⓒ Ⓓ
5 Ⓐ Ⓑ Ⓒ Ⓓ
6 Ⓐ Ⓑ Ⓒ Ⓓ
7 Ⓐ Ⓑ Ⓒ Ⓓ
8 Ⓐ Ⓑ Ⓒ Ⓓ
9 Ⓐ Ⓑ Ⓒ Ⓓ
10 Ⓐ Ⓑ Ⓒ Ⓓ
11 Ⓐ Ⓑ Ⓒ Ⓓ
12 Ⓐ Ⓑ Ⓒ Ⓓ
13 Ⓐ Ⓑ Ⓒ Ⓓ
14 Ⓐ Ⓑ Ⓒ Ⓓ
15 Ⓐ Ⓑ Ⓒ Ⓓ
16 Ⓐ Ⓑ Ⓒ Ⓓ
17 Ⓐ Ⓑ Ⓒ Ⓓ
18 Ⓐ Ⓑ Ⓒ Ⓓ
19 Ⓐ Ⓑ Ⓒ Ⓓ
20 Ⓐ Ⓑ Ⓒ Ⓓ

Directions for marking answers

- Use a No. 2 pencil. Do NOT use ink.
- Make dark marks and bubble in your answers completely.
- If you change an answer, erase your first mark completely.

Right
Ⓐ ⬤ Ⓒ Ⓓ

Wrong
Ⓐ ⊗ Ⓒ Ⓓ
Ⓐ Ⓑ Ⓒ Ⓓ

③ **STUDENT IDENTIFICATION**

0 0 0   0 0   0 0 0 0
1 1 1   1 1   1 1 1 1
2 2 2   2 2   2 2 2 2
3 3 3   3 3   3 3 3 3
4 4 4   4 4   4 4 4 4
5 5 5   5 5   5 5 5 5
6 6 6   6 6   6 6 6 6
7 7 7   7 7   7 7 7 7
8 8 8   8 8   8 8 8 8
9 9 9   9 9   9 9 9 9

Is this your Social Security number?
Yes ⬭   No ⬭

④ **TEST DATE**

MM	D	D	Y	Y
Jan	0	0	200	0
Feb	1	1	200	1
Mar	2	2	200	2
Apr	3	3	200	3
May		4	200	4
Jun		5	200	5
Jul		6	200	6
Aug		7	200	7
Sep		8	200	8
Oct		9	200	9
Nov				
Dec				

⑤ **CLASS NUMBER**

0 0 0 0 0 0 0 0
1 1 1 1 1 1 1 1
2 2 2 2 2 2 2 2
3 3 3 3 3 3 3 3
4 4 4 4 4 4 4 4
5 5 5 5 5 5 5 5
6 6 6 6 6 6 6 6
7 7 7 7 7 7 7 7
8 8 8 8 8 8 8 8
9 9 9 9 9 9 9 9

⑥ **RAW SCORE**

0 0
1 1
2 2
3 3
4 4
5 5
6 6
7 7
8 8
9 9

Life Skills and Test Prep 1
Unit 4 Test Answer Sheet

① _____

    Last Name   First Name   Middle

② _____

    Teacher's Name

TEST

1 (A) (B) (C) (D)
2 (A) (B) (C) (D)
3 (A) (B) (C) (D)
4 (A) (B) (C) (D)
5 (A) (B) (C) (D)
6 (A) (B) (C) (D)
7 (A) (B) (C) (D)
8 (A) (B) (C) (D)
9 (A) (B) (C) (D)
10 (A) (B) (C) (D)
11 (A) (B) (C) (D)
12 (A) (B) (C) (D)
13 (A) (B) (C) (D)
14 (A) (B) (C) (D)
15 (A) (B) (C) (D)
16 (A) (B) (C) (D)
17 (A) (B) (C) (D)
18 (A) (B) (C) (D)
19 (A) (B) (C) (D)
20 (A) (B) (C) (D)

Directions for marking answers

- Use a No. 2 pencil. Do NOT use ink.
- Make dark marks and bubble in your answers completely.
- If you change an answer, erase your first mark completely.

Right
(A) (B) (C) (D)

Wrong
(A) (X) (C) (D)
(A) (B) (C) (D)

③ STUDENT IDENTIFICATION

0	0	0	0	0	0	0	0	0	0
1	1	1	1	1	1	1	1	1	1
2	2	2	2	2	2	2	2	2	2
3	3	3	3	3	3	3	3	3	3
4	4	4	4	4	4	4	4	4	4
5	5	5	5	5	5	5	5	5	5
6	6	6	6	6	6	6	6	6	6
7	7	7	7	7	7	7	7	7	7
8	8	8	8	8	8	8	8	8	8
9	9	9	9	9	9	9	9	9	9

Is this your Social Security number?
Yes ◯   No ◯

④ TEST DATE

MM	D	D	Y	Y
Jan ◯	0	0	200	0
Feb ◯	1	1	200	1
Mar ◯	2	2	200	2
Apr ◯	3	3	200	3
May ◯		4	200	4
Jun ◯		5	200	5
Jul ◯		6	200	6
Aug ◯		7	200	7
Sep ◯		8	200	8
Oct ◯		9	200	9
Nov ◯				
Dec ◯				

⑤ CLASS NUMBER

0	0	0	0	0	0	0	0
1	1	1	1	1	1	1	1
2	2	2	2	2	2	2	2
3	3	3	3	3	3	3	3
4	4	4	4	4	4	4	4
5	5	5	5	5	5	5	5
6	6	6	6	6	6	6	6
7	7	7	7	7	7	7	7
8	8	8	8	8	8	8	8
9	9	9	9	9	9	9	9

⑥ RAW SCORE

0	0
1	1
2	2
3	3
4	4
5	5
6	6
7	7
8	8
9	9

Life Skills and Test Prep 1
Unit 4 Test Answer Sheet

① _____

    Last Name   First Name   Middle

② _____

    Teacher's Name

TEST

1 Ⓐ Ⓑ Ⓒ Ⓓ
2 Ⓐ Ⓑ Ⓒ Ⓓ
3 Ⓐ Ⓑ Ⓒ Ⓓ
4 Ⓐ Ⓑ Ⓒ Ⓓ
5 Ⓐ Ⓑ Ⓒ Ⓓ
6 Ⓐ Ⓑ Ⓒ Ⓓ
7 Ⓐ Ⓑ Ⓒ Ⓓ
8 Ⓐ Ⓑ Ⓒ Ⓓ
9 Ⓐ Ⓑ Ⓒ Ⓓ
10 Ⓐ Ⓑ Ⓒ Ⓓ
11 Ⓐ Ⓑ Ⓒ Ⓓ
12 Ⓐ Ⓑ Ⓒ Ⓓ
13 Ⓐ Ⓑ Ⓒ Ⓓ
14 Ⓐ Ⓑ Ⓒ Ⓓ
15 Ⓐ Ⓑ Ⓒ Ⓓ
16 Ⓐ Ⓑ Ⓒ Ⓓ
17 Ⓐ Ⓑ Ⓒ Ⓓ
18 Ⓐ Ⓑ Ⓒ Ⓓ
19 Ⓐ Ⓑ Ⓒ Ⓓ
20 Ⓐ Ⓑ Ⓒ Ⓓ

Directions for marking answers

- Use a No. 2 pencil. Do NOT use ink.
- Make dark marks and bubble in your answers completely.
- If you change an answer, erase your first mark completely.

Right
Ⓐ ⬤B Ⓒ Ⓓ

Wrong
Ⓐ ⊗ Ⓒ Ⓓ
Ⓐ Ⓑ Ⓒ Ⓓ

③ **STUDENT IDENTIFICATION**

0	0	0	0	0	0	0	0	0
1	1	1	1	1	1	1	1	1
2	2	2	2	2	2	2	2	2
3	3	3	3	3	3	3	3	3
4	4	4	4	4	4	4	4	4
5	5	5	5	5	5	5	5	5
6	6	6	6	6	6	6	6	6
7	7	7	7	7	7	7	7	7
8	8	8	8	8	8	8	8	8
9	9	9	9	9	9	9	9	9

Is this your Social Security number?
Yes ◯ No ◯

④ **TEST DATE**

MM	D	D	Y	Y
Jan ◯	0	0	200	0
Feb ◯	1	1	200	1
Mar ◯	2	2	200	2
Apr ◯	3	3	200	3
May ◯		4	200	4
Jun ◯		5	200	5
Jul ◯		6	200	6
Aug ◯		7	200	7
Sep ◯		8	200	8
Oct ◯		9	200	9
Nov ◯				
Dec ◯				

⑤ **CLASS NUMBER**

0	0	0	0	0	0	0	0
1	1	1	1	1	1	1	1
2	2	2	2	2	2	2	2
3	3	3	3	3	3	3	3
4	4	4	4	4	4	4	4
5	5	5	5	5	5	5	5
6	6	6	6	6	6	6	6
7	7	7	7	7	7	7	7
8	8	8	8	8	8	8	8
9	9	9	9	9	9	9	9

⑥ **RAW SCORE**

0	0
1	1
2	2
3	3
4	4
5	5
6	6
7	7
8	8
9	9

Life Skills and Test Prep 1
Unit 5 Test Answer Sheet

① _____

   Last Name   First Name   Middle

② _____

   Teacher's Name

TEST

1 Ⓐ Ⓑ Ⓒ Ⓓ
2 Ⓐ Ⓑ Ⓒ Ⓓ
3 Ⓐ Ⓑ Ⓒ Ⓓ
4 Ⓐ Ⓑ Ⓒ Ⓓ
5 Ⓐ Ⓑ Ⓒ Ⓓ
6 Ⓐ Ⓑ Ⓒ Ⓓ
7 Ⓐ Ⓑ Ⓒ Ⓓ
8 Ⓐ Ⓑ Ⓒ Ⓓ
9 Ⓐ Ⓑ Ⓒ Ⓓ
10 Ⓐ Ⓑ Ⓒ Ⓓ
11 Ⓐ Ⓑ Ⓒ Ⓓ
12 Ⓐ Ⓑ Ⓒ Ⓓ
13 Ⓐ Ⓑ Ⓒ Ⓓ
14 Ⓐ Ⓑ Ⓒ Ⓓ
15 Ⓐ Ⓑ Ⓒ Ⓓ
16 Ⓐ Ⓑ Ⓒ Ⓓ
17 Ⓐ Ⓑ Ⓒ Ⓓ
18 Ⓐ Ⓑ Ⓒ Ⓓ
19 Ⓐ Ⓑ Ⓒ Ⓓ
20 Ⓐ Ⓑ Ⓒ Ⓓ

Directions for marking answers

- Use a No. 2 pencil. Do NOT use ink.
- Make dark marks and bubble in your answers completely.
- If you change an answer, erase your first mark completely.

Right
Ⓐ ⬤B Ⓒ Ⓓ

Wrong
Ⓐ ⓧ Ⓒ Ⓓ
Ⓐ Ⓑ Ⓒ Ⓓ

③ **STUDENT IDENTIFICATION**

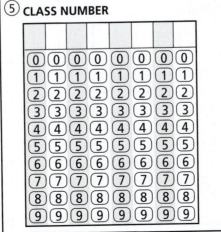

Is this your Social Security number?
Yes ⬭   No ⬭

④ **TEST DATE**

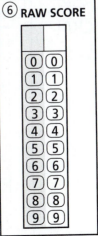

⑤ **CLASS NUMBER**

⑥ **RAW SCORE**

Life Skills and Test Prep 1
Unit 5 Test Answer Sheet

① _____

    Last Name   First Name   Middle

② _____

    Teacher's Name

TEST

1 (A) (B) (C) (D)

2 (A) (B) (C) (D)

3 (A) (B) (C) (D)

4 (A) (B) (C) (D)

5 (A) (B) (C) (D)

6 (A) (B) (C) (D)

7 (A) (B) (C) (D)

8 (A) (B) (C) (D)

9 (A) (B) (C) (D)

10 (A) (B) (C) (D)

11 (A) (B) (C) (D)

12 (A) (B) (C) (D)

13 (A) (B) (C) (D)

14 (A) (B) (C) (D)

15 (A) (B) (C) (D)

16 (A) (B) (C) (D)

17 (A) (B) (C) (D)

18 (A) (B) (C) (D)

19 (A) (B) (C) (D)

20 (A) (B) (C) (D)

Directions for marking answers

- Use a No. 2 pencil. Do NOT use ink.
- Make dark marks and bubble in your answers completely.
- If you change an answer, erase your first mark completely.

Right

(A) (B) (C) (D)

Wrong

(A) (X) (C) (D)

(A) (B) (C) (D)

③ STUDENT IDENTIFICATION

Is this your Social Security number?
Yes ◯   No ◯

④ TEST DATE

MM		D	D	Y	Y
Jan ◯		0	0	200	0
Feb ◯		1	1	200	1
Mar ◯		2	2	200	2
Apr ◯		3	3	200	3
May ◯			4	200	4
Jun ◯			5	200	5
Jul ◯			6	200	6
Aug ◯			7	200	7
Sep ◯			8	200	8
Oct ◯			9	200	9
Nov ◯					
Dec ◯					

⑤ CLASS NUMBER

⑥ RAW SCORE

① _____

Last Name   First Name   Middle

② _____

Teacher's Name

TEST

1 Ⓐ Ⓑ Ⓒ Ⓓ
2 Ⓐ Ⓑ Ⓒ Ⓓ
3 Ⓐ Ⓑ Ⓒ Ⓓ
4 Ⓐ Ⓑ Ⓒ Ⓓ
5 Ⓐ Ⓑ Ⓒ Ⓓ
6 Ⓐ Ⓑ Ⓒ Ⓓ
7 Ⓐ Ⓑ Ⓒ Ⓓ
8 Ⓐ Ⓑ Ⓒ Ⓓ
9 Ⓐ Ⓑ Ⓒ Ⓓ
10 Ⓐ Ⓑ Ⓒ Ⓓ
11 Ⓐ Ⓑ Ⓒ Ⓓ
12 Ⓐ Ⓑ Ⓒ Ⓓ
13 Ⓐ Ⓑ Ⓒ Ⓓ
14 Ⓐ Ⓑ Ⓒ Ⓓ
15 Ⓐ Ⓑ Ⓒ Ⓓ
16 Ⓐ Ⓑ Ⓒ Ⓓ
17 Ⓐ Ⓑ Ⓒ Ⓓ
18 Ⓐ Ⓑ Ⓒ Ⓓ
19 Ⓐ Ⓑ Ⓒ Ⓓ
20 Ⓐ Ⓑ Ⓒ Ⓓ

Directions for marking answers

- Use a No. 2 pencil. Do NOT use ink.
- Make dark marks and bubble in your answers completely.
- If you change an answer, erase your first mark completely.

Right

Ⓐ ⬛Ⓑ Ⓒ Ⓓ

Wrong

Ⓐ ⊗ Ⓒ Ⓓ
Ⓐ Ⓑ Ⓒ Ⓓ

③ **STUDENT IDENTIFICATION**

0 0 0	0 0	0 0 0
1 1 1	1 1	1 1 1
2 2 2	2 2	2 2 2
3 3 3	3 3	3 3 3
4 4 4	4 4	4 4 4
5 5 5	5 5	5 5 5
6 6 6	6 6	6 6 6
7 7 7	7 7	7 7 7
8 8 8	8 8	8 8 8
9 9 9	9 9	9 9 9

Is this your Social Security number?
Yes ⬭ No ⬭

④ **TEST DATE**

MM	D	D	Y	Y
Jan ⬭	0	0	200	0
Feb ⬭	1	1	200	1
Mar ⬭	2	2	200	2
Apr ⬭	3	3	200	3
May ⬭		4	200	4
Jun ⬭		5	200	5
Jul ⬭		6	200	6
Aug ⬭		7	200	7
Sep ⬭		8	200	8
Oct ⬭		9	200	9
Nov ⬭				
Dec ⬭				

⑤ **CLASS NUMBER**

| 0 0 0 0 0 0 0 0 |
| 1 1 1 1 1 1 1 1 |
| 2 2 2 2 2 2 2 2 |
| 3 3 3 3 3 3 3 3 |
| 4 4 4 4 4 4 4 4 |
| 5 5 5 5 5 5 5 5 |
| 6 6 6 6 6 6 6 6 |
| 7 7 7 7 7 7 7 7 |
| 8 8 8 8 8 8 8 8 |
| 9 9 9 9 9 9 9 9 |

⑥ **RAW SCORE**

| 0 0 |
| 1 1 |
| 2 2 |
| 3 3 |
| 4 4 |
| 5 5 |
| 6 6 |
| 7 7 |
| 8 8 |
| 9 9 |

Life Skills and Test Prep 1
Unit 6 Test Answer Sheet

① _____

Last Name   First Name   Middle

② _____

Teacher's Name

TEST

1 Ⓐ Ⓑ Ⓒ Ⓓ
2 Ⓐ Ⓑ Ⓒ Ⓓ
3 Ⓐ Ⓑ Ⓒ Ⓓ
4 Ⓐ Ⓑ Ⓒ Ⓓ
5 Ⓐ Ⓑ Ⓒ Ⓓ
6 Ⓐ Ⓑ Ⓒ Ⓓ
7 Ⓐ Ⓑ Ⓒ Ⓓ
8 Ⓐ Ⓑ Ⓒ Ⓓ
9 Ⓐ Ⓑ Ⓒ Ⓓ
10 Ⓐ Ⓑ Ⓒ Ⓓ
11 Ⓐ Ⓑ Ⓒ Ⓓ
12 Ⓐ Ⓑ Ⓒ Ⓓ
13 Ⓐ Ⓑ Ⓒ Ⓓ
14 Ⓐ Ⓑ Ⓒ Ⓓ
15 Ⓐ Ⓑ Ⓒ Ⓓ
16 Ⓐ Ⓑ Ⓒ Ⓓ
17 Ⓐ Ⓑ Ⓒ Ⓓ
18 Ⓐ Ⓑ Ⓒ Ⓓ
19 Ⓐ Ⓑ Ⓒ Ⓓ
20 Ⓐ Ⓑ Ⓒ Ⓓ

Directions for marking answers

- Use a No. 2 pencil. Do NOT use ink.
- Make dark marks and bubble in your answers completely.
- If you change an answer, erase your first mark completely.

Right
Ⓐ Ⓑ Ⓒ Ⓓ

Wrong
Ⓐ Ⓧ Ⓒ Ⓓ
Ⓐ Ⓑ Ⓒ Ⓓ

③ **STUDENT IDENTIFICATION**

0 0 0 0 0 0 0 0 0
1 1 1 1 1 1 1 1 1
2 2 2 2 2 2 2 2 2
3 3 3 3 3 3 3 3 3
4 4 4 4 4 4 4 4 4
5 5 5 5 5 5 5 5 5
6 6 6 6 6 6 6 6 6
7 7 7 7 7 7 7 7 7
8 8 8 8 8 8 8 8 8
9 9 9 9 9 9 9 9 9

Is this your Social Security number?
Yes ☐   No ☐

④ **TEST DATE**

MM	D	D	Y	Y
Jan ☐	0	0	200	0
Feb ☐	1	1	200	1
Mar ☐	2	2	200	2
Apr ☐	3	3	200	3
May ☐		4	200	4
Jun ☐		5	200	5
Jul ☐		6	200	6
Aug ☐		7	200	7
Sep ☐		8	200	8
Oct ☐		9	200	9
Nov ☐				
Dec ☐				

⑤ **CLASS NUMBER**

0 0 0 0 0 0 0 0
1 1 1 1 1 1 1 1
2 2 2 2 2 2 2 2
3 3 3 3 3 3 3 3
4 4 4 4 4 4 4 4
5 5 5 5 5 5 5 5
6 6 6 6 6 6 6 6
7 7 7 7 7 7 7 7
8 8 8 8 8 8 8 8
9 9 9 9 9 9 9 9

⑥ **RAW SCORE**

0 0
1 1
2 2
3 3
4 4
5 5
6 6
7 7
8 8
9 9

① _____

    Last Name   First Name   Middle

② _____

    Teacher's Name

TEST

1 Ⓐ Ⓑ Ⓒ Ⓓ
2 Ⓐ Ⓑ Ⓒ Ⓓ
3 Ⓐ Ⓑ Ⓒ Ⓓ
4 Ⓐ Ⓑ Ⓒ Ⓓ
5 Ⓐ Ⓑ Ⓒ Ⓓ
6 Ⓐ Ⓑ Ⓒ Ⓓ
7 Ⓐ Ⓑ Ⓒ Ⓓ
8 Ⓐ Ⓑ Ⓒ Ⓓ
9 Ⓐ Ⓑ Ⓒ Ⓓ
10 Ⓐ Ⓑ Ⓒ Ⓓ
11 Ⓐ Ⓑ Ⓒ Ⓓ
12 Ⓐ Ⓑ Ⓒ Ⓓ
13 Ⓐ Ⓑ Ⓒ Ⓓ
14 Ⓐ Ⓑ Ⓒ Ⓓ
15 Ⓐ Ⓑ Ⓒ Ⓓ
16 Ⓐ Ⓑ Ⓒ Ⓓ
17 Ⓐ Ⓑ Ⓒ Ⓓ
18 Ⓐ Ⓑ Ⓒ Ⓓ
19 Ⓐ Ⓑ Ⓒ Ⓓ
20 Ⓐ Ⓑ Ⓒ Ⓓ

Directions for marking answers

- Use a No. 2 pencil. Do NOT use ink.
- Make dark marks and bubble in your answers completely.
- If you change an answer, erase your first mark completely.

Right
Ⓐ Ⓑ Ⓒ Ⓓ

Wrong
Ⓐ Ⓧ Ⓒ Ⓓ
Ⓐ Ⓑ Ⓒ Ⓓ

③ **STUDENT IDENTIFICATION**

Is this your Social Security number?
Yes ☐ No ☐

④ **TEST DATE**

⑤ **CLASS NUMBER**

⑥ **RAW SCORE**

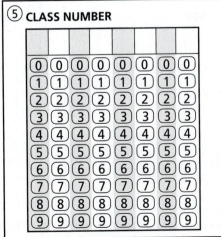

Life Skills and Test Prep 1
Unit 7 Test Answer Sheet

① _____

Last Name   First Name   Middle

② _____

Teacher's Name

TEST

1 Ⓐ Ⓑ Ⓒ Ⓓ
2 Ⓐ Ⓑ Ⓒ Ⓓ
3 Ⓐ Ⓑ Ⓒ Ⓓ
4 Ⓐ Ⓑ Ⓒ Ⓓ
5 Ⓐ Ⓑ Ⓒ Ⓓ
6 Ⓐ Ⓑ Ⓒ Ⓓ
7 Ⓐ Ⓑ Ⓒ Ⓓ
8 Ⓐ Ⓑ Ⓒ Ⓓ
9 Ⓐ Ⓑ Ⓒ Ⓓ
10 Ⓐ Ⓑ Ⓒ Ⓓ
11 Ⓐ Ⓑ Ⓒ Ⓓ
12 Ⓐ Ⓑ Ⓒ Ⓓ
13 Ⓐ Ⓑ Ⓒ Ⓓ
14 Ⓐ Ⓑ Ⓒ Ⓓ
15 Ⓐ Ⓑ Ⓒ Ⓓ
16 Ⓐ Ⓑ Ⓒ Ⓓ
17 Ⓐ Ⓑ Ⓒ Ⓓ
18 Ⓐ Ⓑ Ⓒ Ⓓ
19 Ⓐ Ⓑ Ⓒ Ⓓ
20 Ⓐ Ⓑ Ⓒ Ⓓ

Directions for marking answers

- Use a No. 2 pencil. Do NOT use ink.
- Make dark marks and bubble in your answers completely.
- If you change an answer, erase your first mark completely.

Right
Ⓐ ● Ⓒ Ⓓ

Wrong
Ⓐ ⊗ Ⓒ Ⓓ
Ⓐ Ⓑ Ⓒ Ⓓ

③ STUDENT IDENTIFICATION

0	0	0	0	0	0	0	0	0
1	1	1	1	1	1	1	1	1
2	2	2	2	2	2	2	2	2
3	3	3	3	3	3	3	3	3
4	4	4	4	4	4	4	4	4
5	5	5	5	5	5	5	5	5
6	6	6	6	6	6	6	6	6
7	7	7	7	7	7	7	7	7
8	8	8	8	8	8	8	8	8
9	9	9	9	9	9	9	9	9

Is this your Social Security number?
Yes ◯   No ◯

④ TEST DATE

MM	D	D	Y	Y
Jan	0	0	200	0
Feb	1	1	200	1
Mar	2	2	200	2
Apr	3	3	200	3
May		4	200	4
Jun		5	200	5
Jul		6	200	6
Aug		7	200	7
Sep		8	200	8
Oct		9	200	9
Nov				
Dec				

⑤ CLASS NUMBER

0	0	0	0	0	0	0	0
1	1	1	1	1	1	1	1
2	2	2	2	2	2	2	2
3	3	3	3	3	3	3	3
4	4	4	4	4	4	4	4
5	5	5	5	5	5	5	5
6	6	6	6	6	6	6	6
7	7	7	7	7	7	7	7
8	8	8	8	8	8	8	8
9	9	9	9	9	9	9	9

⑥ RAW SCORE

0	0
1	1
2	2
3	3
4	4
5	5
6	6
7	7
8	8
9	9

Life Skills and Test Prep 1
Unit 8 Test Answer Sheet

① _____

Last Name　　　　　　First Name　　　　　　Middle

② _____

Teacher's Name

TEST

1 Ⓐ Ⓑ Ⓒ Ⓓ
2 Ⓐ Ⓑ Ⓒ Ⓓ
3 Ⓐ Ⓑ Ⓒ Ⓓ
4 Ⓐ Ⓑ Ⓒ Ⓓ
5 Ⓐ Ⓑ Ⓒ Ⓓ
6 Ⓐ Ⓑ Ⓒ Ⓓ
7 Ⓐ Ⓑ Ⓒ Ⓓ
8 Ⓐ Ⓑ Ⓒ Ⓓ
9 Ⓐ Ⓑ Ⓒ Ⓓ
10 Ⓐ Ⓑ Ⓒ Ⓓ
11 Ⓐ Ⓑ Ⓒ Ⓓ
12 Ⓐ Ⓑ Ⓒ Ⓓ
13 Ⓐ Ⓑ Ⓒ Ⓓ
14 Ⓐ Ⓑ Ⓒ Ⓓ
15 Ⓐ Ⓑ Ⓒ Ⓓ
16 Ⓐ Ⓑ Ⓒ Ⓓ
17 Ⓐ Ⓑ Ⓒ Ⓓ
18 Ⓐ Ⓑ Ⓒ Ⓓ
19 Ⓐ Ⓑ Ⓒ Ⓓ
20 Ⓐ Ⓑ Ⓒ Ⓓ

Directions for marking answers

- Use a No. 2 pencil. Do NOT use ink.
- Make dark marks and bubble in your answers completely.
- If you change an answer, erase your first mark completely.

Right
Ⓐ ● Ⓒ Ⓓ

Wrong
Ⓐ ⊗ Ⓒ Ⓓ
Ⓐ Ⓑ Ⓒ Ⓓ

③ STUDENT IDENTIFICATION

Is this your Social Security number?

Yes ◯　No ◯

④ TEST DATE

MM	D	D	Y	Y
Jan ◯	⓪	⓪	200	⓪
Feb ◯	①	①	200	①
Mar ◯	②	②	200	②
Apr ◯	③	③	200	③
May ◯		④	200	④
Jun ◯		⑤	200	⑤
Jul ◯		⑥	200	⑥
Aug ◯		⑦	200	⑦
Sep ◯		⑧	200	⑧
Oct ◯		⑨	200	⑨
Nov ◯				
Dec ◯				

⑤ CLASS NUMBER

⑥ RAW SCORE

Life Skills and Test Prep 1
Unit 8 Test Answer Sheet

① _____

    Last Name   First Name   Middle

② _____

    Teacher's Name

TEST

1 (A) (B) (C) (D)
2 (A) (B) (C) (D)
3 (A) (B) (C) (D)
4 (A) (B) (C) (D)
5 (A) (B) (C) (D)
6 (A) (B) (C) (D)
7 (A) (B) (C) (D)
8 (A) (B) (C) (D)
9 (A) (B) (C) (D)
10 (A) (B) (C) (D)
11 (A) (B) (C) (D)
12 (A) (B) (C) (D)
13 (A) (B) (C) (D)
14 (A) (B) (C) (D)
15 (A) (B) (C) (D)
16 (A) (B) (C) (D)
17 (A) (B) (C) (D)
18 (A) (B) (C) (D)
19 (A) (B) (C) (D)
20 (A) (B) (C) (D)

Directions for marking answers

- Use a No. 2 pencil. Do NOT use ink.
- Make dark marks and bubble in your answers completely.
- If you change an answer, erase your first mark completely.

Right
(A) ●B● (C) (D)

Wrong
(A) (X) (C) (D)
(A) (Ⓑ) (C) (D)

③ **STUDENT IDENTIFICATION**

Is this your Social Security number?
Yes ☐ No ☐

④ **TEST DATE**

MM	D	D	Y	Y
Jan	0	0	200	0
Feb	1	1	200	1
Mar	2	2	200	2
Apr	3	3	200	3
May		4	200	4
Jun		5	200	5
Jul		6	200	6
Aug		7	200	7
Sep		8	200	8
Oct		9	200	9
Nov				
Dec				

⑤ **CLASS NUMBER**

⑥ **RAW SCORE**

Life Skills and Test Prep 1
Unit 9 Test Answer Sheet

① _____
Last Name   First Name   Middle

② _____
Teacher's Name

TEST

1 Ⓐ Ⓑ Ⓒ Ⓓ
2 Ⓐ Ⓑ Ⓒ Ⓓ
3 Ⓐ Ⓑ Ⓒ Ⓓ
4 Ⓐ Ⓑ Ⓒ Ⓓ
5 Ⓐ Ⓑ Ⓒ Ⓓ
6 Ⓐ Ⓑ Ⓒ Ⓓ
7 Ⓐ Ⓑ Ⓒ Ⓓ
8 Ⓐ Ⓑ Ⓒ Ⓓ
9 Ⓐ Ⓑ Ⓒ Ⓓ
10 Ⓐ Ⓑ Ⓒ Ⓓ
11 Ⓐ Ⓑ Ⓒ Ⓓ
12 Ⓐ Ⓑ Ⓒ Ⓓ
13 Ⓐ Ⓑ Ⓒ Ⓓ
14 Ⓐ Ⓑ Ⓒ Ⓓ
15 Ⓐ Ⓑ Ⓒ Ⓓ
16 Ⓐ Ⓑ Ⓒ Ⓓ
17 Ⓐ Ⓑ Ⓒ Ⓓ
18 Ⓐ Ⓑ Ⓒ Ⓓ
19 Ⓐ Ⓑ Ⓒ Ⓓ
20 Ⓐ Ⓑ Ⓒ Ⓓ

Directions for marking answers

- Use a No. 2 pencil. Do NOT use ink.
- Make dark marks and bubble in your answers completely.
- If you change an answer, erase your first mark completely.

Right
Ⓐ ⬤ Ⓒ Ⓓ

Wrong
Ⓐ Ⓧ Ⓒ Ⓓ
Ⓐ Ⓑ Ⓒ Ⓓ

③ STUDENT IDENTIFICATION

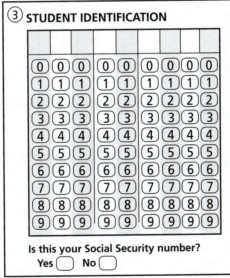

Is this your Social Security number?
Yes ⬭   No ⬭

④ TEST DATE

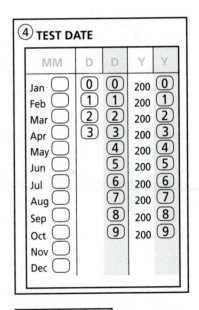

⑤ CLASS NUMBER

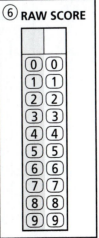

⑥ RAW SCORE

Life Skills and Test Prep 1
Unit 9 Test Answer Sheet

① _____

Last Name   First Name   Middle

② _____

Teacher's Name

TEST

1 Ⓐ Ⓑ Ⓒ Ⓓ

2 Ⓐ Ⓑ Ⓒ Ⓓ

3 Ⓐ Ⓑ Ⓒ Ⓓ

4 Ⓐ Ⓑ Ⓒ Ⓓ

5 Ⓐ Ⓑ Ⓒ Ⓓ

6 Ⓐ Ⓑ Ⓒ Ⓓ

7 Ⓐ Ⓑ Ⓒ Ⓓ

8 Ⓐ Ⓑ Ⓒ Ⓓ

9 Ⓐ Ⓑ Ⓒ Ⓓ

10 Ⓐ Ⓑ Ⓒ Ⓓ

11 Ⓐ Ⓑ Ⓒ Ⓓ

12 Ⓐ Ⓑ Ⓒ Ⓓ

13 Ⓐ Ⓑ Ⓒ Ⓓ

14 Ⓐ Ⓑ Ⓒ Ⓓ

15 Ⓐ Ⓑ Ⓒ Ⓓ

16 Ⓐ Ⓑ Ⓒ Ⓓ

17 Ⓐ Ⓑ Ⓒ Ⓓ

18 Ⓐ Ⓑ Ⓒ Ⓓ

19 Ⓐ Ⓑ Ⓒ Ⓓ

20 Ⓐ Ⓑ Ⓒ Ⓓ

Directions for marking answers

• Use a No. 2 pencil. Do NOT use ink.
• Make dark marks and bubble in your answers completely.
• If you change an answer, erase your first mark completely.

Right

Ⓐ ● Ⓒ Ⓓ

Wrong

Ⓐ ⊗ Ⓒ Ⓓ

Ⓐ Ⓑ Ⓒ Ⓓ

③ STUDENT IDENTIFICATION

Is this your Social Security number?

Yes ◯   No ◯

④ TEST DATE

MM	D	D	Y	Y
Jan	0	0	200	0
Feb	1	1	200	1
Mar	2	2	200	2
Apr	3	3	200	3
May		4	200	4
Jun		5	200	5
Jul		6	200	6
Aug		7	200	7
Sep		8	200	8
Oct		9	200	9
Nov				
Dec				

⑤ CLASS NUMBER

⑥ RAW SCORE

① _____
  Last Name   First Name   Middle

② _____
  Teacher's Name

TEST

1 Ⓐ Ⓑ Ⓒ Ⓓ
2 Ⓐ Ⓑ Ⓒ Ⓓ
3 Ⓐ Ⓑ Ⓒ Ⓓ
4 Ⓐ Ⓑ Ⓒ Ⓓ
5 Ⓐ Ⓑ Ⓒ Ⓓ
6 Ⓐ Ⓑ Ⓒ Ⓓ
7 Ⓐ Ⓑ Ⓒ Ⓓ
8 Ⓐ Ⓑ Ⓒ Ⓓ
9 Ⓐ Ⓑ Ⓒ Ⓓ
10 Ⓐ Ⓑ Ⓒ Ⓓ
11 Ⓐ Ⓑ Ⓒ Ⓓ
12 Ⓐ Ⓑ Ⓒ Ⓓ
13 Ⓐ Ⓑ Ⓒ Ⓓ
14 Ⓐ Ⓑ Ⓒ Ⓓ
15 Ⓐ Ⓑ Ⓒ Ⓓ
16 Ⓐ Ⓑ Ⓒ Ⓓ
17 Ⓐ Ⓑ Ⓒ Ⓓ
18 Ⓐ Ⓑ Ⓒ Ⓓ
19 Ⓐ Ⓑ Ⓒ Ⓓ
20 Ⓐ Ⓑ Ⓒ Ⓓ

Directions for marking answers

- Use a No. 2 pencil. Do NOT use ink.
- Make dark marks and bubble in your answers completely.
- If you change an answer, erase your first mark completely.

Right
Ⓐ ⬤B Ⓒ Ⓓ

Wrong
Ⓐ ⊗ Ⓒ Ⓓ
Ⓐ Ⓑ Ⓒ Ⓓ

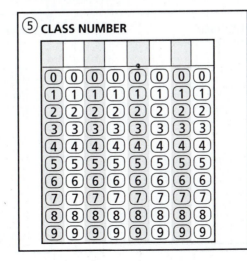

③ STUDENT IDENTIFICATION

Is this your Social Security number?
Yes ☐   No ☐

⑤ CLASS NUMBER

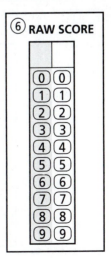

④ TEST DATE

⑥ RAW SCORE

Life Skills and Test Prep 1
Unit 10 Test Answer Sheet

① _____

    Last Name   First Name   Middle

② _____

    Teacher's Name

TEST

1 Ⓐ Ⓑ Ⓒ Ⓓ

2 Ⓐ Ⓑ Ⓒ Ⓓ

3 Ⓐ Ⓑ Ⓒ Ⓓ

4 Ⓐ Ⓑ Ⓒ Ⓓ

5 Ⓐ Ⓑ Ⓒ Ⓓ

6 Ⓐ Ⓑ Ⓒ Ⓓ

7 Ⓐ Ⓑ Ⓒ Ⓓ

8 Ⓐ Ⓑ Ⓒ Ⓓ

9 Ⓐ Ⓑ Ⓒ Ⓓ

10 Ⓐ Ⓑ Ⓒ Ⓓ

11 Ⓐ Ⓑ Ⓒ Ⓓ

12 Ⓐ Ⓑ Ⓒ Ⓓ

13 Ⓐ Ⓑ Ⓒ Ⓓ

14 Ⓐ Ⓑ Ⓒ Ⓓ

15 Ⓐ Ⓑ Ⓒ Ⓓ

16 Ⓐ Ⓑ Ⓒ Ⓓ

17 Ⓐ Ⓑ Ⓒ Ⓓ

18 Ⓐ Ⓑ Ⓒ Ⓓ

19 Ⓐ Ⓑ Ⓒ Ⓓ

20 Ⓐ Ⓑ Ⓒ Ⓓ

Directions for marking answers

- Use a No. 2 pencil. Do NOT use ink.
- Make dark marks and bubble in your answers completely.
- If you change an answer, erase your first mark completely.

Right

Ⓐ ⬤ Ⓒ Ⓓ

Wrong

Ⓐ ⓧ Ⓒ Ⓓ

Ⓐ Ⓑ Ⓒ Ⓓ

③ **STUDENT IDENTIFICATION**

Is this your Social Security number?

Yes ⬭   No ⬭

④ **TEST DATE**

MM	D	D	Y	Y
Jan	0	0	200	0
Feb	1	1	200	1
Mar	2	2	200	2
Apr	3	3	200	3
May		4	200	4
Jun		5	200	5
Jul		6	200	6
Aug		7	200	7
Sep		8	200	8
Oct		9	200	9
Nov				
Dec				

⑤ **CLASS NUMBER**

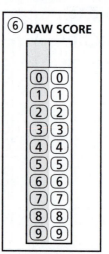

⑥ **RAW SCORE**

Life Skills and Test Prep 1
Unit 11 Test Answer Sheet

① _____
Last Name   First Name   Middle

② _____
Teacher's Name

TEST

1 Ⓐ Ⓑ Ⓒ Ⓓ
2 Ⓐ Ⓑ Ⓒ Ⓓ
3 Ⓐ Ⓑ Ⓒ Ⓓ
4 Ⓐ Ⓑ Ⓒ Ⓓ
5 Ⓐ Ⓑ Ⓒ Ⓓ
6 Ⓐ Ⓑ Ⓒ Ⓓ
7 Ⓐ Ⓑ Ⓒ Ⓓ
8 Ⓐ Ⓑ Ⓒ Ⓓ
9 Ⓐ Ⓑ Ⓒ Ⓓ
10 Ⓐ Ⓑ Ⓒ Ⓓ
11 Ⓐ Ⓑ Ⓒ Ⓓ
12 Ⓐ Ⓑ Ⓒ Ⓓ
13 Ⓐ Ⓑ Ⓒ Ⓓ
14 Ⓐ Ⓑ Ⓒ Ⓓ
15 Ⓐ Ⓑ Ⓒ Ⓓ
16 Ⓐ Ⓑ Ⓒ Ⓓ
17 Ⓐ Ⓑ Ⓒ Ⓓ
18 Ⓐ Ⓑ Ⓒ Ⓓ
19 Ⓐ Ⓑ Ⓒ Ⓓ
20 Ⓐ Ⓑ Ⓒ Ⓓ

Directions for marking answers

- Use a No. 2 pencil. Do NOT use ink.
- Make dark marks and bubble in your answers completely.
- If you change an answer, erase your first mark completely.

Right
Ⓐ ⬛Ⓑ Ⓒ Ⓓ

Wrong
Ⓐ ⊗ Ⓒ Ⓓ
Ⓐ Ⓑ⃝ Ⓒ Ⓓ

③ STUDENT IDENTIFICATION

0 0 0	0 0	0 0 0 0
1 1 1	1 1	1 1 1 1
2 2 2	2 2	2 2 2 2
3 3 3	3 3	3 3 3 3
4 4 4	4 4	4 4 4 4
5 5 5	5 5	5 5 5 5
6 6 6	6 6	6 6 6 6
7 7 7	7 7	7 7 7 7
8 8 8	8 8	8 8 8 8
9 9 9	9 9	9 9 9 9

Is this your Social Security number?
Yes ☐   No ☐

④ TEST DATE

MM	D	D	Y	Y
Jan ☐	0	0	200	0
Feb ☐	1	1	200	1
Mar ☐	2	2	200	2
Apr ☐	3	3	200	3
May ☐		4	200	4
Jun ☐		5	200	5
Jul ☐		6	200	6
Aug ☐		7	200	7
Sep ☐		8	200	8
Oct ☐		9	200	9
Nov ☐				
Dec ☐				

⑤ CLASS NUMBER

| 0 0 0 0 0 0 0 0 |
| 1 1 1 1 1 1 1 1 |
| 2 2 2 2 2 2 2 2 |
| 3 3 3 3 3 3 3 3 |
| 4 4 4 4 4 4 4 4 |
| 5 5 5 5 5 5 5 5 |
| 6 6 6 6 6 6 6 6 |
| 7 7 7 7 7 7 7 7 |
| 8 8 8 8 8 8 8 8 |
| 9 9 9 9 9 9 9 9 |

⑥ RAW SCORE

| 0 0 |
| 1 1 |
| 2 2 |
| 3 3 |
| 4 4 |
| 5 5 |
| 6 6 |
| 7 7 |
| 8 8 |
| 9 9 |

Life Skills and Test Prep 1
Unit 11 Test Answer Sheet

① _____
    Last Name   First Name   Middle

② _____
    Teacher's Name

TEST

1 Ⓐ Ⓑ Ⓒ Ⓓ
2 Ⓐ Ⓑ Ⓒ Ⓓ
3 Ⓐ Ⓑ Ⓒ Ⓓ
4 Ⓐ Ⓑ Ⓒ Ⓓ
5 Ⓐ Ⓑ Ⓒ Ⓓ
6 Ⓐ Ⓑ Ⓒ Ⓓ
7 Ⓐ Ⓑ Ⓒ Ⓓ
8 Ⓐ Ⓑ Ⓒ Ⓓ
9 Ⓐ Ⓑ Ⓒ Ⓓ
10 Ⓐ Ⓑ Ⓒ Ⓓ
11 Ⓐ Ⓑ Ⓒ Ⓓ
12 Ⓐ Ⓑ Ⓒ Ⓓ
13 Ⓐ Ⓑ Ⓒ Ⓓ
14 Ⓐ Ⓑ Ⓒ Ⓓ
15 Ⓐ Ⓑ Ⓒ Ⓓ
16 Ⓐ Ⓑ Ⓒ Ⓓ
17 Ⓐ Ⓑ Ⓒ Ⓓ
18 Ⓐ Ⓑ Ⓒ Ⓓ
19 Ⓐ Ⓑ Ⓒ Ⓓ
20 Ⓐ Ⓑ Ⓒ Ⓓ

Directions for marking answers

- Use a No. 2 pencil. Do NOT use ink.
- Make dark marks and bubble in your answers completely.
- If you change an answer, erase your first mark completely.

Right
Ⓐ Ⓑ Ⓒ Ⓓ

Wrong
Ⓐ Ⓧ Ⓒ Ⓓ
Ⓐ Ⓑ Ⓒ Ⓓ

③ **STUDENT IDENTIFICATION**

Is this your Social Security number?
Yes ⬭   No ⬭

④ **TEST DATE**

MM	D	D	Y	Y
Jan	0	0	200	0
Feb	1	1	200	1
Mar	2	2	200	2
Apr	3	3	200	3
May		4	200	4
Jun		5	200	5
Jul		6	200	6
Aug		7	200	7
Sep		8	200	8
Oct		9	200	9
Nov				
Dec				

⑤ **CLASS NUMBER**

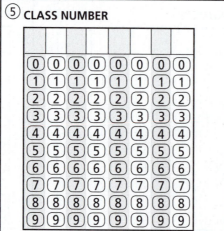

⑥ **RAW SCORE**

Life Skills and Test Prep 1
Unit 12 Test Answer Sheet

① _____
Last Name   First Name   Middle

② _____
Teacher's Name

TEST

1 Ⓐ Ⓑ Ⓒ Ⓓ
2 Ⓐ Ⓑ Ⓒ Ⓓ
3 Ⓐ Ⓑ Ⓒ Ⓓ
4 Ⓐ Ⓑ Ⓒ Ⓓ
5 Ⓐ Ⓑ Ⓒ Ⓓ
6 Ⓐ Ⓑ Ⓒ Ⓓ
7 Ⓐ Ⓑ Ⓒ Ⓓ
8 Ⓐ Ⓑ Ⓒ Ⓓ
9 Ⓐ Ⓑ Ⓒ Ⓓ
10 Ⓐ Ⓑ Ⓒ Ⓓ
11 Ⓐ Ⓑ Ⓒ Ⓓ
12 Ⓐ Ⓑ Ⓒ Ⓓ
13 Ⓐ Ⓑ Ⓒ Ⓓ
14 Ⓐ Ⓑ Ⓒ Ⓓ
15 Ⓐ Ⓑ Ⓒ Ⓓ
16 Ⓐ Ⓑ Ⓒ Ⓓ
17 Ⓐ Ⓑ Ⓒ Ⓓ
18 Ⓐ Ⓑ Ⓒ Ⓓ
19 Ⓐ Ⓑ Ⓒ Ⓓ
20 Ⓐ Ⓑ Ⓒ Ⓓ

Directions for marking answers

- Use a No. 2 pencil. Do NOT use ink.
- Make dark marks and bubble in your answers completely.
- If you change an answer, erase your first mark completely.

Right
Ⓐ ● Ⓒ Ⓓ

Wrong
Ⓐ ⊗ Ⓒ Ⓓ
Ⓐ Ⓑ Ⓒ Ⓓ

③ STUDENT IDENTIFICATION

Is this your Social Security number?
Yes ▢   No ▢

④ TEST DATE

MM	D	D	Y	Y
Jan	0	0	200	0
Feb	1	1	200	1
Mar	2	2	200	2
Apr	3	3	200	3
May		4	200	4
Jun		5	200	5
Jul		6	200	6
Aug		7	200	7
Sep		8	200	8
Oct		9	200	9
Nov				
Dec				

⑤ CLASS NUMBER

⑥ RAW SCORE

Life Skills and Test Prep 1
Unit 12 Test Answer Sheet

① _____

   Last Name   First Name   Middle

② _____

   Teacher's Name

TEST

1 Ⓐ Ⓑ Ⓒ Ⓓ
2 Ⓐ Ⓑ Ⓒ Ⓓ
3 Ⓐ Ⓑ Ⓒ Ⓓ
4 Ⓐ Ⓑ Ⓒ Ⓓ
5 Ⓐ Ⓑ Ⓒ Ⓓ
6 Ⓐ Ⓑ Ⓒ Ⓓ
7 Ⓐ Ⓑ Ⓒ Ⓓ
8 Ⓐ Ⓑ Ⓒ Ⓓ
9 Ⓐ Ⓑ Ⓒ Ⓓ
10 Ⓐ Ⓑ Ⓒ Ⓓ
11 Ⓐ Ⓑ Ⓒ Ⓓ
12 Ⓐ Ⓑ Ⓒ Ⓓ
13 Ⓐ Ⓑ Ⓒ Ⓓ
14 Ⓐ Ⓑ Ⓒ Ⓓ
15 Ⓐ Ⓑ Ⓒ Ⓓ
16 Ⓐ Ⓑ Ⓒ Ⓓ
17 Ⓐ Ⓑ Ⓒ Ⓓ
18 Ⓐ Ⓑ Ⓒ Ⓓ
19 Ⓐ Ⓑ Ⓒ Ⓓ
20 Ⓐ Ⓑ Ⓒ Ⓓ

Directions for marking answers

- Use a No. 2 pencil. Do NOT use ink.
- Make dark marks and bubble in your answers completely.
- If you change an answer, erase your first mark completely.

Right
Ⓐ ⬤ Ⓒ Ⓓ

Wrong
Ⓐ ⊗ Ⓒ Ⓓ
Ⓐ Ⓑ Ⓒ Ⓓ

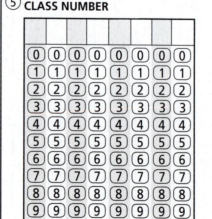

③ **STUDENT IDENTIFICATION**

Is this your Social Security number?
Yes ☐   No ☐

④ **TEST DATE**

⑤ **CLASS NUMBER**

⑥ **RAW SCORE**